Herbert Puchta's 101 Tips for Teaching Teenagers

Cambridge Handbooks for Language Teachers

This series, now with over 50 titles, offers practical ideas, techniques and activities for the teaching of English and other languages, providing inspiration for both teachers and trainers.

The Pocket Editions come in a handy, pocket-sized format and are crammed full of tips and ideas from experienced English language teaching professionals, to enrich your teaching practice.

Recent titles in this series:

Herbert Puchta's 101 Tips for Teaching Teenagers

Herbert Puchta

Consultant and editor: Scott Thornbury

CAMBRIDGE
UNIVERSITY PRESS

CAMBRIDGE
UNIVERSITY PRESS

University Printing House, Cambridge CB2 8BS, United Kingdom

One Liberty Plaza, 20th Floor, New York, NY 10006, USA

477 Williamstown Road, Port Melbourne, VIC 3207, Australia

314–321, 3rd Floor, Plot 3, Splendor Forum, Jasola District Centre, New Delhi – 110025, India

103 Penang Road, #05-06/07, Visioncrest Commercial, Singapore 238467

Cambridge University Press is part of the University of Cambridge.

It furthers the University's mission by disseminating knowledge in the pursuit of education, learning and research at the highest international levels of excellence.

www.cambridge.org
Information on this title: www.cambridge.org/9781108738750

© Cambridge University Press 2021

First published 2021

20 19 18 17 16 15 14 13 12 11 10 9 8 7 6 5 4 3 2

Printed in Great Britain by CPI Group (UK) Ltd, Croydon CR0 4YY

A catalogue record for this publication is available from the British Library

ISBN 978-1-108-73875-0 Paperback
ISBN 978-1-108-73876-7 ebook

Contents

Thanks

I want to thank Scott Thornbury, the series editor, for his constructive and inspiring dialogue on the ideas in this book. A big thank you to Karen Momber and Jo Timerick at Cambridge University Press for their encouragement and patience, and to Alison Sharpe for her editorial precision and many positive comments. Thanks too to the anonymous readers for their suggestions, and to Caroline Petherick for her advice.

Acknowledgements

The authors and publishers acknowledge the following sources of copyright material and are grateful for the permissions granted. While every effort has been made, it has not always been possible to identify the sources of all the material used, or to trace all copyright holders. If any omissions are brought to our notice, we will be happy to include the appropriate acknowledgements on reprinting and in the next update to the digital edition, as applicable.

Text

Tip 62: Activities from *101 Young Adult Novels for Your English Language Class* by Christian Holzmann. Copyright © 2014 Helbling Verlag GmbH. Reproduced with kind permission of Christian Holzmann and Helbling Verlag GmbH; **Tip 70**: "The fireplace is cold, covered with thick ashes," from *One Robe, One Bowl: The Zen Poetry of Ryôkan*, translated and introduced by John Stevens, First edition, 1977. Protected by copyright under the terms of the International Copyright Union. Reprinted by arrangement with The Permissions Company, LLC on behalf of Shambhala Publications Inc., Boulder, CO, www.shambhala.com; **Tip 95**: Excerpt from *Positive Discipline for Teenagers, Revised 3rd Edition: Empowering Your Teens and Yourself Through Kind and Firm Parenting* by Jane Nelsen and Lynn Lott. Copyright © 1994, 2000, 2012 by Jane Nelsen and Lynn Lott. Used by permission of Three Rivers Press, an imprint of Random House, a division of Penguin Random House LLC. All rights reserved.

Typeset

QBS Learning.

Why I wrote this book

I have given seminars on teaching teenagers in a great many countries. At the start of these sessions, I normally ask teachers to engage in three rounds of reflection on their own work with teens. First, I ask them what they find rewarding about teaching teenagers. Typical answers colleagues have come up with include: the opportunities a teen classroom provides for them to respectfully influence young people's development; the fact that teens have general knowledge that teachers often don't (the latest trends in popular culture, for example); teenagers' familiarity with modern technology; their spontaneity and the fun it can be teaching them; and the opportunity to talk about 'real' issues with them and challenge them by discussing solutions to real-world problems.

Following on from that, I ask the participants to list the challenges they regularly come across in their teen classrooms, to compare their answers in pairs and to categorise them. The outcomes of this second round are often amazing. My rough guess is that 90 percent of all the categories of challenges that teachers mention is not about language learning *per se*, or what is usually regarded as language teaching methodology. Rather, it is about the specific challenges presented by the facts that teenagers are going through a phase in their lives characterised by not just a desire to be different from parents and teachers, but also by their search for identity, and the worries, fears and insecurities that come with that. How should teachers cope with these challenges?

In a final round, I ask colleagues to list their specific questions about language teaching methodology in the teenage classroom. I usually get quite a few questions on how to teach the four skills, but also on how to help the learners apply efficient learning strategies and what we can do to help them become responsible adults who have learned to make optimum value-based decisions for themselves in life.

These fascinating and wide-ranging discussions with colleagues over the years have shaped the outline of this book. It is about the methodology of teaching teens – and here we are focusing on the teaching of the four skills. But also it is first and foremost about issues that go beyond language and that have a significant influence on learners' willingness to learn, and the qualities and outcomes of their learning process. In particular, we are looking at motivation, classroom and behaviour management and how we can help foster our learners' maturity. Each of these nine chapters starts with an introduction to the relevant topic and the significance of dealing with it in the teenage classroom.

A look at the literature available on teaching English to teenagers shows that first of all it is scarce, in fact almost non-existent. Secondly, I know of no book that focuses specifically on the issues that quite a few colleagues would seem to need support with. There are, however, some excellent books on what Laurence Steinberg calls the 'New Science of Adolescence'. They deal with educational and psychological issues in the teenage classroom and provide insights based on recent neurobiological research into what goes on in teens' inner world and how that impacts their behaviour and their thinking and feeling.

My own work on teaching teenagers has been significantly influenced over the years by the writing of educational philosopher Kieran Egan. Egan makes the point that a person's intellectual growth happens naturally, through the acquisition of certain intellectual qualities (he calls them 'developments') deeply rooted in our cultural history. In order for an individual's intellect to grow appropriately, the development of certain 'cognitive tools' is essential. The most challenging of these processes is what he calls 'romantic understanding' – a beautiful name, but often a very difficult phase in a young person's life. This is the time when they are overwhelmed with emotions and don't know how to deal with them – with all kinds of consequences for their behaviour and their inner world. In order to move on to 'philosophical development', what is required is the maturation of higher brain functions. It is important to note, however, that these developments are not age-determined; in other words, some young people move into their philosophical thinking frame as late as their twenties or thirties (if at all!).

Fortunately, recent research into teenage development confirms that the teenage years offer great opportunities for us as teachers to influence our learners positively. The tips in this book have been written based on the belief that the problems we so frequently come across in the teenage classroom are challenges that we can overcome and that the changes going on in the teenagers' inner world are opportunities for us to help influence them and guide them towards becoming mature and responsible adults.

I have been involved in teaching teenagers since I started teaching some 40 years ago, first as a teacher in Austria, then as a materials writer, teacher trainer and classroom researcher. Most of the suggestions in this book I have developed and used in various classrooms myself. Others I have learned over the years from colleagues and made 'my own' by adapting them so they fit my own personal style best. I hope you will do the same with the activities in this book that you find useful and want to use in your own classes. I believe they will work best if you too make them your own. This will then help you deal with the more difficult teen developments in a way that feels familiar to you, which will in turn enable you to influence your learners' behaviour – and consequently the classroom dynamics – in the best possible ways.

For readers who would like to immerse themselves more deeply in the fascinating topic of teaching teenagers, I would like to recommend the following books. Not all of them deal with teaching teens directly, but they have had a great influence on my own development and they have informed my thinking and writing over the years.

Arnold, J. and Murphy, T. (Eds.) (2013) *Meaningful Action: Earl Stevick's influence on language teaching.* Cambridge: Cambridge University Press.

Egan, K. (1997) *The Educated Mind: How Cognitive Tools Shape our Understanding.* Chicago: University of Chicago Press.

Egan, K. (2005) *An Imaginative Approach to Teaching.* New Jersey: John Wiley and Sons.

Faber, A. and Mazlish, E. (2006) *How to Talk So Teens Will Listen and Listen So Teens Will Talk.* New York: HarperCollins Publishers.

Meddings, L. and Thornbury, S. (2009) *Teaching Unplugged: Dogme in English Language Teaching.* Peaslake UK: Delta.

Puchta, H. and Schratz, M. (1999) *Teaching Teenagers: Model activity sequences for Humanistic Language Learning.* Pilgrims Longman Resource Books. Longman.

Steinberg, L. (2014) *Age of Opportunity: Lessons from the New Science of Adolescence.* New York: Houghton Mifflin Harcourt Publishing Company.

Stevick, E. (1996) *Memory, Meaning and Method: A View of Language Teaching,* Second edition. Newbury House Teacher Development series: Heinle & Heinle.

Streeck, J., Goodwin, C. and LeBaron, C. (Eds.) (2011) *Embodied Interaction. Language and Body in the Material World*. Cambridge: Cambridge University Press.

Thornbury, S. (2005) *How to Teach Speaking*. Harlow: Pearson Longman.

Zull, J. E. (2002) *The Art of Changing the Brain: Enriching the Practice of Teaching by Exploring the Biology of Learning*. Sterling, VA: Stylus Publishing.

A: Motivation

Teaching teens can be a huge challenge if they can't see how English will be of advantage to them in their future, nor indeed how the learning process itself can engage them and arouse their curiosity. The tips in this section are a balance of serious interactions and elements of surprise, fun and gamification. They will help you not only reach out to your learners through your own enthusiasm, but also create a warm and welcoming classroom atmosphere while you challenge and support them on their individual learning paths.

1 An energy booster to start the lesson
2 Show your enthusiasm
3 Help learners see why learning English is important
4 Make deals
5 Turn the classroom into a special place
6 Gamify learning
7 Teach outdoors occasionally
8 Take your learners' learning seriously
9 Empower learners by asking them to teach *you*
10 Break routines
11 Use rewards artfully
12 Support learners who show self-doubt and negative beliefs

1 | An energy booster to start the lesson

> At the beginning of a class, teens can be sluggish. This activity usually raises their energy levels straight away.

I have frequently used this game as soon as the lesson starts, especially while I'm waiting for a latecomer; they can easily join in without disturbing the class.

- Ask the learners to stand up. Say you will ask them a question, and that those who know the answer can sit down. Although they can cheat by sitting down without knowing the answer, if you suspect that, you will ask them for the answer. If you're right, the game is over for them and they must take their chair to the front of the class and sit on it until a new game starts. If you're wrong, they are still in the game, of course.
- Ask the first question, usually about content from the previous lesson.
- In the first few rounds use some pretty challenging questions, so that not too many learners will get the opportunity to sit down straight away. Also, I don't usually ask a check question then. That raises the suspense and the level of fun for the learners.
- When learners sit down, look at them suspiciously. I do this in an exaggerated way and this usually creates quite a bit of laughter.
- Once everyone is seated, tell them to stand up again. Say that this time if they think they know the answer, they should tell their neighbour.
- Note which of the learners do this, then ask one of them for the answer. If that learner has got the answer right, they can sit down, as can any other learners who have got it right.
- As a follow-up, ask one of the learners still standing in the last round to take over from you and ask questions.
- In a very popular variation of the activity, ask questions about trivia instead of content.
- Yet another variation: one of the learners could ask the questions from the beginning of the activity. (This needs to be set up beforehand.)

Show your enthusiasm

> We know that someone who yawns makes us yawn too.
> But it is less well known that the opposite effect can be
> used to boost our learners' motivation.

Not long ago, I met someone who attended the first English class I
ever taught. 'Do you still like Leonard Cohen?' he asked. 'Yes, I do,'
I replied, intrigued. 'Remember when you brought one of his LPs to
class? I was 13. You were so enthusiastic when you explained this song
to us. My mum always said that we learn for life, not for school – and
that was the first time I understood what she meant.' I thanked him
for the compliment and felt quite embarrassed. Because, to the best of
my memory, my first few years of teaching were filled with trial and
error (with an emphasis on error); not a lot to write home about! But I
have always shared my enthusiasm for the subject with my learners. A
lucky strike indeed – from the very beginning I got something right that
research now shows is essential for motivating learners!

Mercer and Dörnyei (2020) say that, 'If teachers are engaged and
passionate about their work and their languages, then learners are more
likely to be too.' So:

- Show your passion for your subject. Use books, songs, images, realia
  and anecdotes to make your enthusiasm tangible. You can even
  exaggerate a bit. Nobody has ever complained about their teacher
  being too passionate!
- I occasionally say, 'Oh, I love this word,' when writing a new word
  on the board. Then I repeat it as if tasting something scrumptious
  and suggest what they can do with it. Of course some teens will say
  things like, 'But you love *every* word!' or imitate your enthusiasm,
  which usually leads to laughter.
- Sometimes, when I teach a concept new to them, I tend to say things
  like, 'This is an important moment. Understanding this is important
  for your future lives. Not many adults understand this.'

Mercer, S. and Dörnyei, Z. (2020) *Engaging Language Learners in Contemporary
Classrooms*. Cambridge: Cambridge University Press. Kindle Edition.

3   Help learners see why learning English is important

> As teachers we need to 'sell' our learners the idea that what we are teaching them will be of advantage to them.

One of the biggest problems for me as a young teacher in rural Austria was to help my learners find a satisfactory answer to the question, *Why am I supposed to learn English?* But these days, things have changed dramatically – many teenagers have contact with English outside their classroom through technology, social media and the web.

A good way of getting learners to reflect on their own motivations to learn English is a Consensogram. (For more on this, see the reference below.) Write up a series of statements or adapt these:

- If I succeed in learning English, I will have better opportunities to study and get a good job.
- People who have a good command of English are often admired.
- Once I'm at university, most of my reading will be in English.
- By learning English I might lose touch with my own culture and traditions.
- English is useful for playing online games.
- The better I can communicate in English, the more fun it'll be to interact with people from other countries and cultures.
- The time spent learning English takes time away from other important subjects.

Ask learners to express their opinion about each statement by giving three points (*I totally agree.*), two points (*This is kind of important for me.*) and one point (*I don't agree at all.*). Hand out coloured dots. Ask learners to stick them on a large piece of poster paper and create a rating scale in the form of a bar chart.

Ask your learners to work in pairs and discuss these questions: *What do you notice when you look at the data? What surprises you? What are your conclusions?*

Stobaugh, R. (2019) *50 Strategies to Boost Cognitive Engagement. Creative Thinking in the Classroom.* Bloomington, IN: Solution Tree Press.

Make deals

> **If you offer a good deal to a class of teens – or to an individual learner – you are likely to impress them.**

I guess it's with tongue in cheek that Nelsen and Lott (2012) say, 'Since teens can be so self-centred and expect the world to revolve around them, making deals can motivate them when all else fails.' But actually, whether it's teens' self-centredness or – as I suspect – that they feel surprised and respected when we offer them a deal, deals do work! Teens perceive deal-making as cool, something that normally happens between peers. But with a teacher? Wow!

A bad deal is something like, *We'll watch this film if you promise to prepare really well for the test.* We're giving them something now, and afterwards we have no leverage. And if the test results are disappointing, it's too late anyway.

So, offer time-sensitive deals: promise learners something if they do something by a certain time. *Last week you used your own language twenty-three times in my class. If you can get this down to a maximum of 12 by Thursday, we'll play X* (the game they really like) or *we'll watch a clip from Y* (the movie or series they really like). Or: *I'll do you a deal. We'll do a project about American rap music if you find another teacher who's willing to join us with their class.* You offer something motivating, and learners commit to taking action from the outset. By expecting them to persuade another teacher to join the project, you demonstrate your trust in them.

Sometimes it's good to write a deal down and have it signed by everyone. That makes the deal more 'official' and shows how seriously you take it (and your learners). Don't offer anything expensive; your offering a deal is often more important than what they actually get. Humour helps, too. For example, invite learners to lunch. On the day, put up a sign: '(Your name)'s restaurant'. Then have a picnic in the school grounds.

Nelsen, J. and Lott, L. (2012) *Positive Discipline for Teenagers 3rd edition.* Potter/Ten Speed/Harmony/Rodale. Kindle Edition.

5 Turn the classroom into a special place

> Your learners spend a lot of time in the classroom. Make sure it offers a positive learning environment that they like coming into.

Success in the language class depends mainly on what goes on '… inside and between the people in the classroom,' as Stevick (1980) pointed out. But other qualities – for example, whether the classroom itself looks and feels inviting – are important too, especially for teens.

- Giving learners a say and listening to their suggestions about changes you might make to their learning environment, even if they are small ones, can make a lot of difference. Have a suggestion box and encourage learners to use it to contribute ideas.
- Display a motivational quote on the classroom wall, e.g. *The happiest people don't have the best of everything; they just make the best of everything.* Leave it there for a few days before you ask learners to comment on it from their own point of view. Replace the quote with a new one after a week, or – even better – ask learners to find a new one.
- Ask learners to contribute to a 'role model of the month' project. Learners work in groups to prepare a poster on a special person who could be a role model. Ask them to research that person's life story, and to state on the poster why he or she is a role model for them. Each group then presents their role model, and the learners vote to decide which of the posters goes up on the wall.
- Assign responsibilities (such as furniture arrangement, waste disposal, board cleaning) to individual learners on a rotating basis.
- Make sure the classroom is pleasing. Ask learners to help you decorate the room; for example, flowers can change the atmosphere significantly, and so can colours.

Stevick, E. (1980) *Teaching Languages: A Way and Ways.* Rowley, MA: Newbury House.

Gamify learning

> We need passion and commitment from our learners. To instil those attitudes, add gaming to the learning.

Teens love digital games. They are all about being challenged and getting rewards, with elements of chance. Dopamine and endorphins are released. The excitement grows and the players feel good.

In an ideal classroom, all learners will be intrinsically motivated – they find learning fun, interesting and rewarding. But while our learners may be intrinsically motivated to do certain things, they won't necessarily be keen on English. So gaming elements can be helpful.

- Get a soft-tip/magnetic dartboard. Create question categories: content from previous lessons, sport, films, grammar, lexis, etc. Match each category with a section on the dartboard. For each category, write questions on index cards and points for the correct answer. Form pairs. A throws a dart, B draws a card from the respective pile. Play for, say, 10 minutes at the end of a lesson.
- Help learners gamify their home study. Write a to-do list at the end of a lesson, with points for each task. Before the next lesson, learners write their points on a wall chart. To add a chance element, draw a learner's name, then play *Paper, scissors, stone* with them and award points for beating you. That is hugely motivational.
- A chore can become a game. If studying a list of spellings, for example, they give themselves points: the faster they learn, the more the points. But they deduct points for using their phone while studying. This only works if they're honest with themselves!
- Establish two teams. Write/Project two choices on the board, one of them correct (e.g. spelling, *believe/beliefe*; or grammar, *she taught/ she teached*), for the learners to call out the correct one.

'Games and Your Brain: How to Use Gamification to Stop Procrastinating', https://buffer.com/resources/brain-playing-games-why-our-brains-are-so-attracted-to-playing-games-the-science-of-gamification

7 Teach outdoors occasionally

> You might like to surprise your learners by suggesting a lesson outside the classroom – but with a clear plan in mind for meaningful language work.

Tell your learners that you believe it's possible to focus on work outside the confines of the classroom (assuming parental and institutional permission). It is advisable to take your learners to a safe location that's not too noisy, e.g. a nearby park.

- Ask learners to take pen and paper with them. Tell them to walk round for about 10 minutes with an open mind about anything they notice. Give them questions to answer, e.g. *What did I notice? What did I see, hear, touch, smell?* Ask learners to find a comfortable spot and write a short text on their findings. In the next lesson, ask them to read out their texts to each other, and talk about them.
- Tell your learners a few days beforehand that you are going to take them to a place where they might meet a lot of English-speaking people; this could be, for example, an airport, a train station or a tourist attraction. Get learners to work in pairs and discuss questions they could ask people they meet there. Help them with language they need, especially on how to open a conversation and introduce themselves. You could also get them to film the interviews on their phones, but make sure they know how to ask permission to do that. Learners could then work on a report and present their findings to the class.
- If your learners have access to a class or school library, why don't you encourage them to pick a book and start reading it outside? Make sure they choose a place that will facilitate their reading process. This could be followed up with a discussion afterwards on whether their choice was a good one and what other favourite reading places they have.
- Tell learners to walk around in pairs and have a chat – on one condition only. They have to speak English, while the topic of the conversation is totally up to them.

> Ironically, when showing learners that we take their learning seriously, in order to be credible we often have to start by taking *them* seriously – as individuals with their own personalities – and not simply as learners of a language.

Zoltán Dörnyei (2001) points out that if we '... show commitment towards the learners' learning and progress, there is a very good chance that they will do the same thing'. He lists a range of ways we can use to show our learners that we are committed to their learning, from caring for them when things don't go well, to correcting and returning their homework and tests promptly, to sending them links to articles they may find interesting, and even to giving them our phone number to call us at home when they have a problem. (If the latter is one step too far for you, you might like to consider giving them your email address.)

I once offered a teenage class an hour of extra time per week outside the regular timetable, to help them with learning problems. These after-class sessions were very successful; they became quite popular, and felt a bit like a bonding experience. Things did get a bit tricky one day, though, when my learners asked me to help them with a maths problem as they had a test the next day. I'd not exactly excelled at maths myself, but was lucky enough to be able to help them with that particular question. Phew!

Make sure you set up regular sessions when your learners can share their true thoughts and opinions – ideally with them sitting in a circle. Be non-judgemental; this doesn't mean that you need to find all their conclusions equally valid, but that when you disagree with anything one of them says, do so respectfully. Try to ask questions that encourage your learners to think more deeply and express their thoughts. Do not accept them merely stating, for instance, 'I don't like that'; tell them to give their reasons.

Dörnyei, Z. (2001) *Motivational Strategies in the Language Classroom*. Cambridge: Cambridge University Press.

9   Empower learners by asking them to teach *you*

> There is always going to be at least one learner in your class who's better than you at something. Invite your learners to find out what those things are, and to teach you about them.

Giving your learners a chance to teach you something new has several advantages:

1 It makes you human, and at the same time raises their self-esteem – after all, it gives them an opportunity to demonstrate to you something they are good at which you may have never found out about otherwise!
2 You can be absolutely sure that the level of engagement in your class will be high and there'll probably be a lot of fun and laughter.
3 You can demonstrate to them what the joy of learning something new looks like.

- Ask learners to interview you in order to find out about their areas of expertise in which you are a beginner: rap music, the ins and outs of the latest smartphone technology, a language they speak and you don't, a sport they play – it doesn't really matter. What counts is that they find something to teach you!
- Once learners have an idea of what that might be, tell them to work in groups. Ask each group to plan how they would go about creating a mini-lesson for you. Ask them to check the web for videos or other materials that might help them with the language they need to do their task.
- You may want to give the other learners observation tasks for each group's mini-lesson. These could be drawn up together, and could include questions about you and the way you learn, the 'teacher' and the way they teach, and everyone's feelings during the lesson.
- Make sure learners can share their observations afterwards. Don't forget to thank your learners for their efforts in teaching you – and do tell them what you enjoyed about being taught by them!
- As a variation, you could encourage learners to teach something to the whole class that only they are an 'expert' in.

Break routines

> Routines are important, as they help to save planning time. But too much routine can create boredom. Occasionally breaking routines can boost learners' motivation.

I have used the following rule-breaking ideas successfully with teenage learners:

- Hand out a short 'letter' to each learner at the beginning of your lesson informing them how this one will be different from many other lessons. I have, for example, told my learners that I'm going to be absolutely silent in this lesson, and asked them to observe how this changes the nature of the classroom. If you do this, whenever you want to communicate something to them, you'll need to use mime and gestures, or write short instructions on the board. Make sure you finish the experiment a few minutes before the lesson ends so you can discuss it with your learners.

- Tell your learners at the beginning of the class that each time you give them a signal (e.g. ring a bell), every person in the class, including you, is going to take two minutes to write down their inner monologue at that stage of the lesson. Make sure they know what an inner monologue is, and maybe show them an example that you have written. Ask them to number their short texts for ease of reference later on. At the end of the class, ask volunteers to read out their inner monologues, and share yours, too.

- At the beginning of the class, ask a learner to swap seats with you. Ask that learner to sit at your desk for the whole lesson, while you start the lesson sitting at their desk, and return to it several times during the lesson.

- A similar idea is to use a teaching spot very different from your usual one; for example, if you tend to stand in front of the class most of the time, try standing at the back.

Dörnyei, Z. (2001) *Motivational Strategies in the Language Classroom*. Cambridge: Cambridge University Press.

11 Use rewards artfully

> Rewards work best when they come as a surprise to learners, not something they are entitled to if they have achieved something or behaved well.

In his book *Punished by Rewards*, Kohn (2018) points out that while the traditional carrot-and-stick approach along the lines of, 'If you do X, then you'll get Y,' may create behaviour that pleases the teacher temporarily, it is not a sustainable educational strategy. This is because if teenagers do their work in order to get rewarded, there is the danger that the reward – rather than the learning process itself – becomes their main interest. As a consequence, some of them might even go as far as cheating in order to get rewarded.

In contrast, I have often noticed that unexpected rewards, i.e. not given as part of a *quid pro quo* routine, can have a strong motivational impact on individual learners or indeed a whole class, and can make a great contribution towards creating a friendly classroom culture. Here are some tips for using rewards:

- Don't promise rewards as incentives for 'good' behaviour. Use rewards as surprises, rather, to acknowledge special efforts you see having been made.
- If at all possible, personalise your rewards. If you know that one of your learners is into, for example, windsurfing, give them a list of links to articles they may find interesting.
- I have very successfully used a glass jar and pebbles with learners of all age groups. Whenever a learner says something spontaneously in English and makes a great contribution to the class conversation, ask them to add a pebble. Once the jar is full, surprise your class, e.g. tell them a story, organise a games lesson or show them a video (and don't forget the popcorn!).
- Occasionally – for example at the end of a successful term, or when learners have presented the outcomes of a project they have been working on hard – celebrate their achievement together with them.

Kohn, A. (2018) *Punished by Rewards: The Trouble with Gold Stars, Incentive Plans, A's, Praise, and Other Bribes. 25th Edition.* Boston: Houghton Mifflin Harcourt.

Support learners who show self-doubt and negative beliefs

> Self-doubt can be demotivating, and damage our learners' self-esteem. A healthy level of self-doubt, on the other hand, can be important for learners' motivation.

When one of your learners shows signs of self-doubt, it might be an idea to talk to them individually first. Make sure they understand that self-doubt can be useful at times; without it we would always feel we're right, and we would be less motivated to learn. But also tell them that too much self-doubt can be problematic because it makes it impossible for us to accept or even see our qualities, so can block us from achieving anything.

- Share with your learners a story of when you failed at something. Tell them how you felt, and how you dealt with the situation. This can be empowering for your learners – they can feel their teachers are brilliant at just anything.
- Tell your learners that research has shown that self-kindness can help us overcome self-doubt. Encourage them to make it a routine to write down at the end of each day three things that they did well.
- Ask your learners to list (individually, or in pairs, supporting each other) what they are good at outside class. Tell them to forget about school for a time and be generous to themselves in finding those strengths.
- Get learners to do a bit of internet research to find stories of highly successful people who were not good at school or who failed many times before they became famous. They are very likely to come across Einstein, who apparently was unable to speak until he was four and a half, and only started reading when he was almost eight. Other examples would include Beethoven, Walt Disney and Elizabeth Holms.

B: Classroom management

Classroom management is about techniques, skills and strategies you can use in order to help your learners work in a focused, efficient and academically organised way. Without that, the classroom would be a place so chaotic as to make it very difficult, impossible even, for learners to pay attention and learn effectively. The tips in this section address ways of managing the class (both the room and its occupants) in order to optimise learning.

Activate your learners right from the start

> You may once have been told that you shouldn't start
> the lesson without every learner paying attention. That
> can be tricky!

Have you ever entered the classroom and noticed your learners are
anything but ready for the lesson? Some may not have taken their books
out, and others may not even have taken their coat off. If you were to
face individual learners and say something along the lines of, 'I'm not
going to start the lesson unless you take your coat off!' the situation
might develop into a wild west kind of showdown. This is because teens
want to be in control and complying with what you have just told them
to do would mean losing face in front of their classmates.

I have found that it works best to ignore the lack of readiness and
instead engage learners in a simple activity straight away. Here are
some ideas:

- Work with a partner and write down 10 words that you learned in
  the last lesson.
- Think of a text you read or listened to in the last lesson. Write three
  sentences stating what you learned from the text, and three questions
  you have about the content of the text. Write a short text (for your
  teacher/for a classmate) beginning: 'Did you hear/see/read about …?'
- Write three sentences with the first word in each of them starting
  with the letter *A* (choose any letter, but not *J*, *Q*, *X* or *Z*; they are
  too rare in English).
- Think of six sentences, each containing a word you recently learned.
  Write up the sentences, but leave that one word out of each sentence.
  Give them to a partner to complete.

It is now time for you to walk round, observe what learners are doing
and signal to individuals that you are happy with their performance. If a
learner has still got their coat on, give them a nod and quietly ask them
to take it off.

14　Start the lesson with attention

> The sooner you can engage your learners in a thinking task, the better they will be able to pay attention. And sometimes it's important to calm them down.

Here are a few suggestions for activities you can use to quickly engage and settle your learners:

- **A quote:** At the beginning of the class write up a quote, e.g. Shonda Rhimes's *You can waste your lives drawing lines. Or you can live your life crossing them.* Tell your learners that you will ask them for their thoughts on this at the end of the class.
- **Pre-questions:** Studies have shown that the retention rate is higher when learners are asked pre-questions. Try writing a question (or two or three) on the board about the content that you will be dealing with in the lesson. Ask your learners to choose at least one of the questions and write their answer(s) on a slip of paper with their name on it. Collect the strips of paper. At the end of the class, come back to the learners' answers and get them to compare these with what they have learned in the lesson.
- **Timers and thank-yous:** At the start/end of an activity, when you want to calm your learners, give them a visual countdown, either on your fingers, starting at five, counting down, or even better, if you have a projector in your classroom, project decreasing numbers down to zero. It's important that you yourself are focused and calm so learners will understand that you expect the same from them. The more you 'freeze', the better you will be as a model for them! Alternatively, when you are standing in front of the class waiting for learners to calm down, name individual learners and thank them. *Thank you, Manuelle, for being calm. Great, thanks for joining in, Claire. Now I need three more people to become calm. I'm not saying your names. You know who you are … .*

Carpenter, S. K. and Toftness, A. R. (2017) The Effect of Prequestions on Learning from Video Presentations. *Journal of Applied Research in Memory and Cognition* Volume 6, Issue 1, 104–109.

Establish classroom routines

> Classroom routines can save time, and require the learners' active participation: the more they understand the need to take their responsibilities seriously, the easier it will be to establish a classroom culture they want to belong to.

To establish a routine, we need to provide a good reason for it. And then we need to be persistent and patient. If you notice your learners becoming sloppy, elicit the reasons for the routine, and the routine itself, e.g. *I wonder who can still remember what you need to do about your homework? – Put it on your desk? – That's right, and when? – At the beginning of the class.* (thumbs up sign) – *Remember why I insist on this routine? – It saves time.* (thumbs up sign), etc.

It's good to have a routine for the beginning of the class. I often start lessons by asking about words or phrases they learned in the previous class: *Give me five words or phrases that have to do with X. Give me six words that describe people's feelings*, etc.

It can be a challenge to establish calm after a group activity. So tell your learners that when group work is over, you'll raise your hand, and get them to agree that as soon as they see that, they will raise theirs, too, and stop talking. This has a nice unifying effect – and is much more effective than you trying to cut through the noise with your voice.

Sometimes it's good to agree on gestures as a means of communication. Pointing your two index fingers against one another could stand for *pair work*, for example. Moving the fingers of both of your hands in a circling motion might signal that you want your learners to mill around to ask and answer questions. Describing a circle with one hand could suggest that you want them to sit in a circle, etc.

It's good to end the class with a routine. Asking learners what they have learned in the lesson makes them aware of their progress and provides feedback for you, too. Questions could be: *What are the things you learned today? Was there anything you learned today that surprised you?* etc.

16   How to use the walls of your classroom

> I must confess that for a long time I didn't really give much thought as to how the walls of the classroom could be used to support my learners' learning. Now I realise their value.

Teenagers pay attention to visuals, so I'm introducing the term *psychogeography*. It refers to the effect the organisation of a place has on how the people in it feel and behave. The walls of a classroom are a large part of its psychogeography, so they are likely to have a big impact on the quality of the learning that takes place within them.

Weinstein and Novodvorsky (2015) observe: 'Classrooms too often resemble motel rooms. They are pleasant but impersonal, revealing nothing about the people who use the space.' You can appear much more approachable if you personalise a bit of wall space. So:

- Photos of yourself as a student may trigger interest in what school life was like for you. Souvenirs from a trip you've taken, photos of yourself and your family, and cartoons or jokes will make learners curious about you and create a congenial impression of you.
- Photos you have taken of your learners at school events and printed out show your interest in them.
- Newspaper clippings, inspiring quotations and posters reflecting positive values, as long as you rotate them regularly, might motivate learners to read and think.
- It's good to have a world map for cultural references.
- You might want to allocate part of the classroom wall to learners' own displays. Tell them that what they put up must contribute positively to their learning and if not, you might have to remove it.
- Display texts written by learners but make sure they're happy about that. If not, or if the classroom is used by other classes, they could write their name on the back of the paper or use a nickname.

Weinstein, C. S. and Novodvorsky, I. (2015) *Middle and Secondary Classroom Management: Lessons from Research and Practice 5th edition.* McGraw-Hill Higher Education. Kindle Edition.

Enlarge your action zone

> When the seating arrangement in a classroom is in rows,
> there is an obvious action zone – learners nearer to the
> teacher seem to be more active than those in the back rows.

Teachers who tend to stand in front of the class are more likely to
activate learners in the two or three front rows. It seems that a distance
of four or five metres from the teacher creates some kind of action
border; learners sitting outside of that line tend to be less active.

Is that because learners who are more eager to participate pick a seat
nearer to the teacher, or do we activate other learners less? As Weinstein
and Novodvorsky (2015) state, research hasn't found the definitive
answer to these questions yet, but they do quote a student saying,
'When we're all so close to the front, you know that the teacher can see
you real easily. That helps keep you awake!'

We have various options as to how we can improve the situation:

- One is to rotate learners frequently. Put up a list that shows the
  learners the changes that will take place over time, e.g. a semester. That
  way all you need to do is remind them at the end of each week about
  the change next week. This can save you a lot of instruction time.
- If you walk around the classroom, the action zone will move around
  with you. Learners will hear your voice from different directions,
  and learners sitting at the back will feel more involved.
- In phases where you decide to be in front of the classroom for a
  longer time (for example during storytelling), make sure you give
  more eye contact to the learners further away from you.
- Do not always wait for learners to participate voluntarily. Another
  way to expand or vary the action zone is by calling them by name
  and asking them to contribute. That avoids a lot of waiting time too.

Weinstein, C. S. and Novodvorsky, I. (2015) *Middle and Secondary Classroom
Management: Lessons from Research and Practice 5th edition.* McGraw-Hill Higher
Education. Kindle Edition.

18 Arrange learners in groups for a reason

> The seating arrangement in your class is important; choose it carefully and adapt it to your lesson plan.

While travelling and giving talks, I've had the pleasure and the privilege of sitting in on teenage and young learners' classrooms in many countries. This has shown me a lot of teacher passion and learner engagement. One point that often surprises me, though, especially in secondary schools, is that I sometimes find the furniture arranged in groups, but in the lesson nothing happens to make use of that. When I ask questions about it, the standard answer tends to be that 'teens like that'. While I have no doubt this is the case, I don't think this is reason enough for a static arrangement of chairs and desks in groups. I believe that seating arrangements need to be decided mindfully.

- When you plan your lesson, go through your notes and, as though creating a film, see in your mind learners working and interacting in the various phases of your lesson. For each phase, ask yourself what would work best – learners directing their attention towards the front of the class, working in groups, in pairs, or individually? Or would it be better to have them milling around the classroom and interacting with other learners?
- Then consider the time required to make changes to the furniture (assuming it's not fixed in place). Ask yourself how you can train your learners to make changes rapidly and quietly. Ask yourself what kind of arrangement might be one that allows for changes most easily; space permitting, I have found pairs of desks arranged in a V-shape very flexible. All learners can easily focus on the board and can work in pairs or individually without making any changes, and when group arrangements are needed, the changes require almost no time.

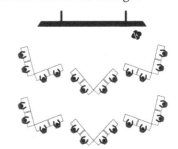

Use visual anchors

> Visual signals or anchors can be very useful for managing
> the dynamics of the classroom efficiently. They save time,
> and give learners a sense of security.

Observe your classroom dynamics and come up with your own visual
signals to support your communication with your class. For example,
when working with 14-year-olds I explained why it would be much
better to use English only as a medium of communication in the
classroom. They agreed with my reasons. However, they kept falling
back into their mother tongue. So I made a flag of an English-speaking
country with the words 'English spoken' on it. I asked them to fix the
sign on the outside of the classroom door. I explained that I wanted
this to be a sign to the world outside that our classroom was English-
speaking territory. The class had great fun when one day the science
teacher came into the class to make an announcement. 'You must speak
English!' the learners shouted, and to their delight, the teacher complied
with the rule!

It's sometimes difficult for learners to know whether they can make
mistakes (for example, during a roleplay activity), or when they are
supposed to focus on getting a form right (e.g. during a drill). To help
them become more aware of the difference, I suggest using icons. When
you put a flag showing a 😊 on the board, this will signal to your
learners that the focus is on *fluency*, so it doesn't matter if they make
mistakes. The other icon, a thinking face 🤔, stands for *accuracy* and
tells them you want their focus to be on correct form. But there are
times, too, to put both flags on the board (for example, when revising a
roleplay).

Another idea is for when you might find it difficult to get your learners
to calm down after a high-energy activity. You could go to the board
and write a *P* on it, then say, 'This stands for please sit down again and
pay attention.'

20 Make lessons flow

> It's great when learners are surprised when a lesson is over. But lessons can drag along forever, too. What's the difference that makes the difference?

I remember one of my teacher trainees with a class of young teens. She wrote a sentence on the board. She asked learners to call out words they associated with it and created a mind map with them. Then she told the class to use it to write a story. Half of the learners started writing immediately. But two learners were still calling out words. Then a boy announced, 'I left my note block at home!' The trainee looked for some paper. And a girl asked, 'Must we use all the words?' By the time several learners had shouted 'Finished!' others hadn't even started.

In the 1970s, Kounin carried out breakthrough research into how teachers' actions influence learners' behaviour. A key insight he gained was that disruptions in the flow of a lesson can often be avoided proactively, if teachers know how to act *before* these occur. Here are key dos and don'ts for maintaining flow:

- **Do** make sure transitions between activities are smooth: tell learners when an activity is over; wait a moment; then explain the next one. In a situation such as the one with my trainee teacher above, the teacher could say: *OK. Please put your hands down. Thanks. Please use some of the words to write a story now. You've got five minutes for this. Lisa, what do you have to do?* (Girl repeats instruction.) She quickly asks another learner to help out with note paper. *OK. Start writing, please. Five minutes.*
- **Don't** let yourself get distracted from the lesson flow. If somebody acts in an unhelpful way, use gestures to signal you're determined to go on – and don't waste any time by commenting on the interruption.
- **Don't** break up an activity into bits (Kounin called this 'fragmentation') when it can be carried out in one go. Don't over-explain, nor talk too much – those interrupt the flow as well.

Kounin, J. S. (1970) *Discipline and group management in classrooms.* New York: Holt, Rinehart and Winston.

Establish an online learning buddy system

> For safety reasons, scuba-divers always dive with a
> 'buddy'. In the teenage classroom, buddies can support
> each other in preparing for tests and exams.

Learning buddy systems are popular with teenagers because they
create a link between classroom and home and can be of great help,
especially – but not only – for those learners who, the further they are
from school, the lower their incentive is to learn. Plus, buddy testing is
one of the most efficient study strategies.

- You need to consider how best to pair up your learners:
  academically stronger learners with ones who need more support;
  learners who complement each other in character; ones with similar
  interests, etc.
- Tell learners that the learning buddy system will help them support each
  other in preparing for exams and tests and will be more interesting and
  fun. So they will need to start meeting up regularly online a few weeks
  prior to exams, using their favoured form of social media.
- Let's say there is a list of words/lexical chunks to study for a test. At
  first, the two learners work together, creating a series of sentences
  containing the lexical items. Then they test each other: A says one of
  the sentences, leaving out the word or chunk they are learning, with
  no hint as to the whereabouts of the gap in the sentence; B has to
  correctly complete the sentence from memory. Then they swap roles.
  It's a challenging task that requires some thought, and helps learners
  build up substantial lexical knowledge. Done regularly, this will
  develop their memory skills as well.
- Your learners can also, of course, prepare for grammar and skills
  tests in buddy pairs. Go through some examples of test types and
  show them how best to test each other in pairs.

The advantage of buddy learning, when it works well, lies in the fact
that learners appreciate working together and supporting each other,
so will be learning important life competencies at the same time and,
what's more, it can be a lot of fun!

Make sure learners do what YOU want them to do

> Teens can be pretty creative about finding excuses for not doing what we have asked them to. So, when giving instructions, it's good to be proactive.

This means three things: you need learners to pay full attention to your instructions, your instructions need to be clear, and you want learners to confirm they have understood you.

- The first thing you need to do is create silence. Stand calmly in front of your class, with your feet slightly apart, and don't move. Be congruent. If your aim is to get your learners to sit still, moving around is counterproductive. If you can – smile.
- Tell learners the reason why you want them to do things the way you specify.
- Use precise instructions. Don't say *Write a short text* – if a learner wants to provoke you, they might only write one sentence. (*But you said a short text!*) Rather, say: *I want you to write a text of 80 to 100 words*.
- Make sure learners have understood you. Ask, e.g. *Tom, can you tell me what you're supposed to do now?*
- If you feel a particular learner needs a bit more direction from you, you can follow up by asking them how they would go about doing the task you have given them. You could say, e.g. *Tom, can you show me how you would start doing …?* Stay with that learner for a bit of time and help them if necessary. Once they can see they are on the right track, they will be much more likely to complete the task.
- You may well decide that you want to give this kind of extra guidance by talking to the learner quietly, directly and privately, so you don't disturb the other learners (who may be working on the task already).

Don't let your voice become high-pitched or loud

> Your learners need you to be in control, especially when noise levels are high. The way you come across then is crucial.

When you want your learners to refocus after group work, you may find it difficult to be heard. You may feel the need to speak louder, but that might cause them to talk louder, too. (They don't want their conversations interrupted!) Speaking loudly may strain your throat, and if your voice becomes high-pitched you risk appearing ridiculous. So, how can you create the impression that you are in control?

- In order to attract learners' attention, non-verbal communications expert Michael Grinder suggests you break through the noise – but only briefly. Shout, 'Class!' for example, clapping your hands twice or three times. Then freeze and keep completely quiet for two or three seconds. Then carry on talking to the class at a lower volume of voice than usual. Try this out – you may be surprised by how well it works.
- I have occasionally simply written an instruction on the board – again, after a freeze phase. While writing with your back to the class, you may need to turn around and freeze again if they are not paying attention.
- Sometimes it's enough to talk loudly, then drop your voice down to a near-whisper. The secret of this strategy seems to be that you lower your voice gradually – so learners can follow you, until they are completely quiet. Then smile – that smile indicates that it's you who is in control!
- Very rarely, I use another of Grinder's strategies, the 'disciplining spot' – a place in the classroom I only go to when I need to air my frustration about something or somebody. I never tell my learners about it but it seems they intuitively sense that when I go there, there is reason for them to behave. But I would never stand there to praise them. That would create psychogeographical pollution! (See **16**.)

C: Classroom culture

I use the term 'classroom culture' as discussed by Breen (1986) in addressing the complexity of the interactive and social aspects of the classroom; he portrays this complexity as a coral reef with its surface hiding a multiplicity of life forms and challenges. 'Most often the flow of classroom life is actually under the surface. What is observable is the rim of a socio-cognitive coral reef! Classroom life seems to require that many learners spend surprising amounts of time doing little, whilst a teacher spends equally surprising amounts of time trying to do too much.' Hopefully, the tips in this section will help you discover some of the hidden challenges, and explore ways of meeting them successfully (without having to do too much!).

24 Create a classroom culture your learners want to belong to
25 Show learners you care for their physical well-being
26 Establish the ground rules together
27 Inject some light-hearted fun into the lessons
28 Help learners cope with stress
29 Deal with errors wisely
30 Help your learners learn from their mistakes
31 Ask for feedback
32 Take learners' emotions seriously
33 Make learners feel they are in control

Breen, M. P. (1986) The social context of language learning – a neglected situation. *Studies in Second Language Acquisition* 7: 135–58.

Create a classroom culture your learners want to belong to

> The way you interact with your learners has a significant impact on how welcome they feel.

As a young teacher, I was told by a 14-year-old who I had taught for several years that she had thought at first that I wasn't very nice because when I entered the classroom for my very first lesson with her class, I 'looked grumpy'. I was surprised because I'm not normally seen as bad-tempered. With hindsight, she had probably caught me at a moment when I was deep in thought, unaware of the difference a smile would have made to my learners.

- You never get a second chance to create a first impression. In a class for the first time, smile and make eye contact with all learners.
- Make sure you know learners' names, and use them. Use mnemonic techniques to memorise them, e.g. create an association or rhyme between a person's name and an object the name reminds you of, then a picture that fuses the two. If a learner is called Sue, think of, e.g. *Sue in a zoo*, and remember a picture of her climbing a giraffe's (super-long) neck.
- Keep a 'Getting to know your learners' file. In it, note personal things about them. Use them in small talk.
- Reserve part of a classroom wall or free web-space to display texts your learners have written.
- Some teachers make a point of greeting learners at the classroom door; shaking their hands and telling them it's good to see them.
- Or, if you can, be in the classroom when the learners arrive and greet each one as they enter. Also, related to this, don't make a big deal about latecomers; just let them quietly enter and integrate as quickly as possible into the classroom dynamic.
- Show learners you like teaching them. Even if that isn't a hundred percent true, pretend to do so; a bit of positive pretence can really change the classroom atmosphere for the better, and – magically – can often change your own perception of a difficult class, too!

25 Show learners you care for their physical well-being

> Learners' physical well-being has a direct influence on their motivation and their emotional well-being.

- Check the room temperature. Air it if another group has just been using the same room.
- If the furniture is movable, check how chairs and desks are distributed so no one is crammed into a corner and sightlines are optimal.
- Make sure learners have water bottles. A study shows that most teens drink too little water and that can affect their fatigue levels.
- Negotiate clear rules as to what foods learners may bring into class, and where helmets, phones, etc. should be stowed.
- Get learners out of their seats at least once during a lesson:
  1. Do a milling activity: learners walk round and talk at random.
  2. Ask your learners to stand up and do a minute of pizza breathing: they imagine holding a slice of pizza on the palm of their hand. They inhale the delightful aroma of the pizza through their nose, and then blow slowly on the pizza to cool it down.
  3. When learners are over-excited, use a creative visualisation activity to calm them down. (For a rich source of creative visualisation activities see the reference below.)
- Have a game ready for low-energy moments. One of my favourites is 'Don't answer'. The learners stand in a circle. One learner goes up to another and asks them a question, e.g. *Where would you most like to be right now, Mario?* That learner must not reply, but the learner on their left answers for them. They can completely make it up, of course. This usually creates laughter!

Arnold, J., Puchta, H. and Rinvolucri, M. (2007) *Imagine That! Mental imagery in the EFL classroom.* Helbling Languages.

Establish the ground rules together

> Rules are important for living together. Most teens will understand that.

Tell learners that you want to establish fair ground rules for the classroom together with them. Say that you will accept any of their suggestions if it helps make the classroom a better place and you will make suggestions, too. Also tell them that a clear majority vote for any particular rule means it will be passed and everyone has to accept it.

Ask learners in groups to brainstorm ideas under these two headings:

Problems in our class / Rules we should introduce

Set five minutes for this phase and ask one learner in each group to be the spokesperson, to write down keywords for each suggestion that comes from the group and report on the group findings afterwards.

Before each spokesperson shares their report, ask the class to take notes under three headings: *I agree / I don't agree / A question I have*

When the learners have heard the suggestions, it's time for you to add yours. Then tell them to comment on the suggestions and vote on each of them. Whenever a suggestion for a rule has a clear majority, make a note of it and tell the learners that this rule will be implemented.

Have a big sheet of poster paper ready for the next class with the ground rules written on it, and enough space for everyone to sign it. After all the signatures have been added, pin it up on the wall.

Make sure you remind learners of the rules whenever necessary. Be prepared for your learners to refer to the rules, too, if you do not act in accordance with one of them!

This tip is based on an idea in the reference below.

Puchta, H. and Schratz, M. (1999) *Teaching Teenagers: Model Activity Sequences for Humanistic Language Teaching 5th edition*. London: Longman.

27 Inject some light-hearted fun into the lessons

Not every teacher is a born comedian. And learning is a serious business, isn't it? Yet if we can laugh with our learners every now and then, the classroom will be a better place.

It has been shown that laughter strengthens the immune system, is good for our cardiovascular health, releases endorphins and hence eases stress. We don't have to be comedians to put a smile on our learners' faces. Can we learn to be funny? Well, we can at least try. Here are some ideas:

- If you look serious most of the time, try wearing a pair of crazy sunglasses or a T-shirt with a silly slogan on it. You may notice a smile on your learners' faces – you can develop that into a bit of laughter by laughing about yourself with them.
- Peter Medgyes, the author of *Laughing Matters*, always puts on a jester's cap and bells as a signal that he's going to tell a joke. That already creates laughter – even among ELT teachers.
- Try telling learners a joke – the internet is full of them (and some of them are really good!). If they don't find it funny, use a bit of irony – teens usually love that, especially when it's directed at yourself, e.g. *Aren't I brilliant at telling jokes? Normally everybody rolls on the floor when I tell one.*
- Of course, the best laughs are often the unanticipated, e.g. the teacher's (kind) enactment of what a learner's error (e.g. 'Mum's in the chicken' instead of 'kitchen') actually means. Clearly, there's a narrow line between ridicule and good-natured fun, and between sarcasm and teasing. We need to tread that line carefully until, at least, we know our learners really well.
- Invite learners to prepare some jokes to share in the next lesson. It only takes two or three minutes – time well spent!
- Watch a Charlie Chaplin movie with learners. Get them to construct the dialogue, or reconstruct the story.

Medgyes, P. (2002) *Laughing Matters: Humour in the Language Classroom*. Cambridge: Cambridge University Press.

Help learners cope with stress

> If we take our teens' stress seriously, they are likely to have
> more respect for us.

Stress is common in teens, and their stress levels can equal or surpass those of adults. The main stress factors for teens include worries about school, their family, their relationships, their future and the world. Common behavioural outcomes are lack of sleep, over- or undereating, eating unhealthy foods, and feeling exhausted, angry, nervous or overwhelmed.

We can help learners deal with stress if we are non-judgemental about what causes it (e.g. errors) and empathetic to their situation (see **29** and **30**). With teens who are reluctant to talk about themselves, I have found that starting with content unrelated to their own situation usually helps break the ice. For example, you could suggest to them that they use a search engine to find an article about teens and stress in another country, e.g. by searching "teens+stress+<country name>". Ask them to read and compare the situation with their own. That will probably trigger a lively discussion among higher-level learners. Allow the discussion to be held in their own language if needed. (If you don't understand it, ask a good learner to mediate for you.)

Another strategy is a positive thoughts journal. For this, learners' homework is to write at least 100 words every day on positive topics. Give them examples, e.g. a kind deed someone did for them or someone else; a place that gives them positive energy; a person who supports them. It's good if you write a journal, too.

Other 'stress-busters' include telling jokes (see **27**); TPR (for relaxation); sharing 'a good thing that happened recently'; diagramming and sharing 'my support network'; silent reading solely for pleasure; non-competitive games.

There is a whole chapter with a wide range of practical suggestions aimed at easing teenagers' and young adults' stress in the ELT classroom in the reference below.

Williams, M., Puchta, H. and Mercer, S. (2021) *Psychology in Practice*. Innsbruck: Helbling.

29　Deal with errors wisely

> Most learners will tell you that they want to know their mistakes. However, to work well, error correction needs to be done in a constructive and sensitive manner.

Teens can be very touchy. So even if some of us feel frustrated when learners make mistakes, especially in areas that they 'should know by now', we need to avoid coming across as judgemental or disappointed with their language errors. Such reactions can lead to silence in the classroom. When you teach (post) beginners, or take over learners that have learned English for several years but don't yet speak autonomously, don't correct much. Be patient and understanding, nod your head to indicate you understand their struggle, and scaffold their production. Correct discreetly. (L: *I scaring of snakes.* T: *Ah, you're scared of snakes. Me too. I'm scared of snakes.*)

When learners speak more confidently, do correct them. Indicate if something is not clear. (L: *My sister is thirty years old.* T: *Thirteen or thirty?* noting both numbers on board.) Sometimes it's useful to point out the grammatical concept rather than the form. (L: *... and then we going to the park.* – T: *Past simple* – L: *Yes, we went to the park. There was ... .*)

Don't interrupt discussions or roleplay activities too often. Give learners delayed feedback, either individually (giving learners notes pointing out what they did well and a few errors they made). Or use whole-group discussions. (T: *Somebody said, 'Where's better at football – Tom or Ken?' Is that correct?*)

Do correct wrong forms when drilling, or – much better – get learners to correct themselves. Imagine you are drilling the present perfect for completion and ask learners to form sentences with 'I've ...'. If a learner forms an incorrect sentence, say: *That's not quite correct. Think about it.* Indicate that they can quietly ask other learners for help, too. Learners usually have no problem asking others for help.

Help your learners learn from their mistakes

> When teens have done something wrong, the last thing
> you want is to make them feel guilty or ashamed. Instead,
> show them how to learn from their mistakes.

Teens tend to blame others or the circumstances for things that have
gone wrong, or they become defensive about their behaviour and block
themselves from gaining insights into how things went wrong. You can
facilitate a different kind of behaviour by being frank about mistakes
you have made. Then learners can see how to deal with mistakes in
a constructive way. Nelsen and Lott (2012) recommend using 'The
four R's of Recovery from Mistakes', Recognition, Responsibility,
Reconciliation and Resolution.

Tell learners a story of a mistake you made, e.g. as a student you were
asked by the science teacher to carry a piece of equipment back to the
lab but you dropped it. You tried to cover it up, hoping the teacher
wouldn't notice the damage. For some time, you avoided thinking of
the incident, but felt awful about it. So you decided to own up. To your
surprise, the teacher was very understanding. She even thanked you for
telling her. Say what you learned from that: it doesn't pay to lie about
a mistake; it's much better to own up. You could also use the story of a
mistake you made as the basis of a dictogloss activity (see 77 on how to
do this).

Go through the story with your class. Ask learners to match the four
Rs to the different stages of the narrative. Share your experience that
everybody makes mistakes. Ask learners for examples of mistakes
friends (or they themselves) have made. Discuss with them how using
the 4 Rs strategy could help in such situations. Encourage them to use
the strategy. From time to time, have them discuss in pairs how the
strategy works for them. Depending on the level of your learners, these
discussions may require the use of the learners' own language.

Nelsen, J. and Lott, L. (2012) *Positive Discipline for Teenagers Revised 3rd Edition.*
New York: Penguin Random House.

Ask for feedback

> Encouraging learners to share their perceptions of the teaching and learning process can help you understand better how you can make your teaching even more efficient.

Involving learners in feedback discussions requires a culture of mutual trust. In order to establish that, it's important to share with your learners the reasons why you want feedback from them on your teaching. Giving feedback can help learners feel more responsible for their own learning.

- Watch carefully what happens when you ask questions such as: *Do you understand?* I have often noticed that it's not enough if a few of my learners say *yes* or nod their heads. Note the ones who don't react at all. Wait a bit and observe their body language, then ask each of those learners, e.g. *What are the things you'd like me to help you with?*
- Hand out three pieces of coloured paper for traffic light feedback. Tell learners: *Green means fine; amber OK, but some problems; red means not OK.* Ask: *How well are you getting on with your work?* e.g. while learners are working in groups. Make sure you attend first to the groups showing you red cards, then turn to the ones with the amber ones.
- Occasionally, ask learners for a quick sign on how interested they are in the lesson. Both hands on their desk would mean *I'm not interested at all*, while holding one hand high above their head could stand for *I'm totally interested.* Then ask further questions to find out more, e.g. *Please share with us what stops you from being more interested. / If you were the teacher, what changes would you make to arouse more interest?* etc.
- Put up a feedback box near the door. Encourage learners to write on a slip of paper a sentence or two that tells you what they would like you to know about the lesson you've just given them. Make sure you thank learners for doing this as they do it, and read what they have said afterwards – in a non-judgemental manner.

Take learners' emotions seriously

> Young teens in particular can be overwhelmed with emotions. So it is worth learning strategies that can help you to help them.

It can be difficult to respond helpfully when learners air their frustration. Let's assume you've just given them some homework when suddenly one of them bursts out, *This is ridiculous! We've got a maths test coming up, and now you're giving us so much homework!* Standard teacher answers often lead to conflict: *You should have started studying for that test earlier, then the homework I'm giving you wouldn't be any problem!* Advice comes from Faber and Mazlish. They say that although it doesn't always sound like it, teens want to know where we stand and what our beliefs and values are, so they can take them into consideration when making decisions. Hence, we first need to assure them that we've listened to them and understand how they feel before calmly conveying our viewpoint. So instead of telling them off for not wanting to do your precious homework, try one of the following:

- Separate emotions from intentions: *I see. Sounds like you're pulled in two directions. You want to make sure you do well in your maths test, and you can't see how to fit in the homework I've just given you.*
- Invite learners to see the issue from your perspective: *I hear what you're saying and I understand. I wonder what you'd say if you were me.*
- Accept learners' emotions – giving your reasons: *I hear how much you'd prefer not to have to do any homework in English at all right now. The problem is I need you to write this story as we'll start the next lesson with all of you reading each other's texts.*
- Use 'what if': *Yeah, I know. Wouldn't it be great if I never had to set any homework? You'd think I was the world's best teacher.*

Faber, A. and Mazlish, E. (2006) *How to Talk So Teens Will Listen and Listen So Teens Will Talk*. New York: HarperCollins Publishers.

Make learners feel they are in control

> Not having any control over a situation is a terrible feeling
> for an adolescent. So every now and then, make sure your
> learners get the feeling that they are in control.

When I started teaching teens, my main concern was that I might not be able to control them. So I used a lot of 'control language': *Raise your hands before you speak! Stop writing now. Quiet, please!* etc. But there is evidence that too much control and strictness can be damaging for adolescents' emotional health. The neurobiologist James Zull says, 'No outside influence or force can cause a brain to learn. It will decide on its own. Thus, one important rule for helping people learn is to help the learner feel she is in control. This is probably the best trick that teachers have.'

If we want to follow this advice, we need to be cautious. Giving our learners too much control too early generates the risk that they will be overwhelmed by having to make decisions. It is better to give *some* power to them, gradually, and in a carefully structured way. Here are some ideas for how to go about doing this:

- Give learners small choices first: *Do you want to do Exercise 3 first, or Exercise 4? Do you want to revise for the test now, or at the end of the lesson?*
- Encourage individual learners to make choices. *We've got five minutes left – Sandra, please choose how we could spend them.*
- Every now and then, create a plan for a lesson (for several lessons, or a whole week) learners can do independently. List a series of instructions they have to follow. It's up to each learner to decide what order they want to tackle them in. Put up a solutions sheet somewhere on the wall so they can check their answers. Don't forget to include open-ended creative tasks, too. (See also **8** and **26**.)

Zull, J. E. (2002) *The Art of Changing the Brain: Enriching the Practice of Teaching by Exploring the Biology of Learning.* Stylus Publishing.

D: Listening

Understanding a new language can be a huge challenge, especially for those whose sense of self-esteem is fragile. This is why we need to help our learners get into a focused yet relaxed state of mind, and one in which they feel ready to understand the gist of a text, whether fact or fiction, without an inner voice telling them they can't do it. Listening with a partner, interactive listening activities and listening games are just some of the scenarios we can provide to develop a range of strategies that help with listening tasks.

34 Teach learners to listen out for keywords

> Having to understand the main ideas in demanding texts can be stressful for teens, and that can block their comprehension.

I have used the following strategies to help learners become focused yet relaxed while listening:

- Give learners a handout with a word cloud of, say, 10 to 12 keywords from the listening text, including two or three words that are not. Give them a few minutes to create sentences using the words.
- Tell learners you're going to play an audio text or a video. Ask them to listen/watch and circle the words they hear. Ask learners to work in pairs and create a short summary of the audio/video, drawing on the keywords and their memory.
- Then, ask the pairs to list some questions they have about the content. Ask them to call them out. Write the questions on the board and play the audio/video again.
- Ask learners for any specific comprehension problems. If there are any words, phrases or sentences they don't understand, play the relevant parts of the audio several times so they get a chance to understand without stress. Praise them for their effort in listening several times.

I have successfully used another variation of the keywords technique when revising stories. Start by asking learners to call out words from the story that you have told them or they have listened to in the previous lesson, and write each one of them on the board. Make sure you have plenty of words, at least one per learner. Then allocate a word to each learner. If there are more words, give each learner a second or even a third word. Ask them to listen to the story one more time, and whenever they hear one of their words they should get up, go to the board and point to it, then immediately sit back down, focusing on the listening again.

This is a popular activity as, although it does demand concentration, it allows learners to get out of their seats occasionally as well.

> **When learners listen to a story, they need to decode key language, and in order to comprehend the story, they need to create a representation of the story in their mind.**

Learners need to understand the setting, the characters and the sequence of events as the story unfolds, so storyboarding can be helpful.

A storyboard is often used for planning animated film. It consists of a sequence of drawings – in the style of a simple comic strip rather than a more sophisticated graphic novel – and contains text for directions and occasionally also bits of dialogue.

I usually introduce the idea of storyboarding (see the reference below) after listening to a story with my learners. I go to the board, and say: *OK, let's draw the story now*. I start by drawing a few frames on the board and then ask the learners questions: *OK, so what's in the first frame of the story? Where are we? Who are the characters? What are they doing?* While the learners call out their answers, I start drawing, in a very simple matchstick style. The more we get into the story, the more I try to elicit from the learners by asking questions, sometimes saying something myself that is clearly wrong to encourage them to 'correct' me. I develop the story like this, frame by frame. I have often found that learners get quite involved – they especially like the fact that their teacher takes the risk of drawing on the board in front of them in spite of a clear lack of artistic talent – and at the same time I can see how well they have understood the story. Those who haven't yet understood bits of it get help from the others and from the sketches on the board. So the technique works as a safety net for learners who have not understood very well, and it offers good formative feedback – learners can see, without feeling judged, how well they are doing with understanding narratives.

Harmer, J. and Puchta, H. (2018) *Story-Based Language Teaching*. Helbling.

Use various ways of dictating texts

> Dictations are often seen as old-fashioned. You may want
> to rediscover them – they can be a lot of fun.

It seems that for learners with spelling issues the more traditional
dictations they have to take, the more insecure they become. Here are
some ways to make dictations fun and helpful:

- Visual dictations: poor spellers often write what they hear, and in
  English this is counterproductive. So teach learners to remember
  what words look like. Write difficult words on strips of paper. Hold
  up a word and ask learners to memorise it. Then take the word
  down and ask learners to write it. Hold the word up again for
  learners to check. Repeat regularly.
- Pre-teach some simple commands such as: *Repeat the word/sentence,
  please. Speak more slowly. Can you spell that? Speak up, please.* Then,
  having told the learners to use the commands if necessary, dictate a
  short text, sometimes talking a bit too fast or using a low voice.
- Pair dictations: write a text on a computer. Copy it to make two
  versions. Put blanks into the two texts by changing the colour of
  alternating word groups to white:

A: Usually,	B: , sleeping on the
is a big problem	job for an
– if you ,	employee – fall asleep,
you'll be fired. ...	. But ...

In pairs, learners reconstruct it by dictating it to each other.
- Running dictation: put four texts on the wall, and put learners in
  groups. One learner from each group runs to their text, remembers a
  sentence, runs back, dictates it, then it's another learner's turn.
- Quadruple dictations: put the class into four groups; each gets a dictation
  from one group member standing at the far wall. Chaos? It usually
  develops into deep concentration as learners focus, despite the noise!

Rinvolucri, M. and Davies, P. (1989) *Dictation: New Methods, New Possibilities.*
Cambridge: Cambridge University Press.

The super statement challenge

> **Teens love challenges, especially when they involve pair work.**

Memory tasks, problem-solving activities and decision-making challenges are all super-motivating for teens. This is an example of a listening activity combining those features, with a gaming element (see **6**).

Preparation: find an intriguing short text or image. Write a list for yourself of 20 statements about it, using language you have taught recently and want to review. Some of the statements should be false. Mark one of them as your 'super statement'. You can choose totally randomly, or pick a sentence on purpose as an important language model.

- Hand out a copy of the text/picture to each pair, or project it. Tell learners to remember as many details about it as possible in, e.g. three minutes. Encourage them to talk to each other during this phase – this helps them remember the details. Then tell them to put the text/image face down on their desk (or black out the projection).
- Tell learners to listen carefully because you'll be reading out – just once – 20 sentences about the text/picture – some false. The pairs have six minutes to remember the sentences and write them in one of two columns (*True/False*).
- Pairs get two points for each statement correctly listed, and another two per statement in correct English. They don't have to remember the exact wording, though.
- Say they will only find out later which is the 'super statement'. If that's among their sentences and in the right column (*True/False*), that's ten bonus points, and another ten if they've got the language right.
- Read the sentences. Collect the papers. Redistribute them, so the pairs can check each other's results. Go through the sentences with them. Tell them to add up the points. Only then do you announce the super statement. (I recently used a recording of a drum roll to raise their excitement.) Ask them to add the super statement points.
- If you repeat this game over time, keep a results list on the classroom wall. Write the names of the pairs on strips of coloured paper and stick them to the list, to update the order.

Motivate learners to listen attentively to each other

> Learners often listen to other learners less attentively than they do to you. When that happens, there are some strategies you can use to increase their level of attention.

Listening requires 'paying attention' – an interesting metaphor that suggests that when we are focused, we need to give something in order to get something else. So, what do learners have to give, or give up, in order to get more out of their learning process?

They need to give up their butterfly mind while they're learning. They need to stick to whatever they are learning for a certain amount of time – they cannot just let their minds wander and engage in other things simultaneously. They have to limit their socialising, chatting to others, moving about, etc. We can support learners by praising them for the effort of listening, and by modelling good listening behaviour. Here are some ideas for ways of encouraging attentive listening:

- Ask learners how we know that somebody is listening to us carefully when we tell them something, although they don't say much. Elicit non-verbal strategies, such as eye contact, nodding the head, etc. and verbal strategies such as: *Mmm … Yes …, Go on … .*
- On a piece of poster paper, write language that's useful for the listener's active participation, e.g.
  Summarising: *So, what happened was …*
  Showing empathic emotions: *Wow! / Really? How sad! / Great! / Awesome. / Cool!*
  Asking questions: *What happened next? / Why do you think he did that?*
- Ask learners to prepare a one-minute speech on a topic important to them. Offer to listen to a trial run, and give them feedback to improve their performance. Tell them to write six quiz questions about the content of their speech. Then ask the class to work in groups and take turns giving their speeches. One learner gives their speech, the others focus on committing to memory as much content as possible, and at the same time use the strategies from above to show they're listening. When the presenter has finished, ask them to dictate the questions to the others. Finally, they compare their answers.

Try Rogerian listening to improve communication in class

Teens – like many adults – often listen without paying proper attention. We can help learners learn to listen actively.

The famous psychologist Carl Rogers developed a technique, named after him, which teaches people how to listen. The listener summarises, at intervals, what the speaker has said, to check their understanding of the message. The speaker corrects as necessary. Far from being a memory task requiring the listener to repeat verbatim, it develops alertness in the listener, respect between speaker and listener, and better communication all round.

In the ELT classroom, higher-level learners (B1 upwards) can use this technique to improve their listening skills. This works best when based on an opinion gap – when the speaker starts to express their thoughts and beliefs about a certain situation or action, and the listener doesn't yet know how the speaker is going to continue. Here is an activity to practise the technique:

- Cut out a newspaper photo or headline that is likely to trigger a brisk discussion among your learners. It might refer to the current topic in their coursebook. Stick it on an A4 sheet of paper. Draw 10 to 12 speech bubbles around it and write statements in them expressing opinions on the topic.
- Give each learner a copy of the handout. Tell them to read it and think about it. Make sure they understand the language. Tell them to make notes about their own opinions. Walk round the class to help if needed.
- Ask learners to work in pairs. A states their opinion. B listens attentively and sums up A's opinion as they understand it, using questions such as *OK, so do you think ...?* A can either confirm correct understanding, or explain more if they feel what B has said does not adequately reflect what they have said. The pair carry on until they come to an agreement. Then B says whether they agree or disagree with A's opinion, and explains why. A listens and then summarises their understanding of what B has said, etc.
- After some time ask learners what they have learned from this activity.

Rogers, C. R. and Farson, E. E. (1957) *Active Listening*. Martino Publishing.

40 Use collective listening to raise learners' level of attention

> Learners will listen in a focused way if they know that it'll be their turn to speak soon, as is the case in collective storytelling.

The idea is simple: one person starts telling a story, and continues until they get a certain signal. Then somebody else picks up the story, etc. This technique encourages learners to listen attentively and the fact that the story is a collaborative effort is usually a motivating factor, too.

This technique works particularly well if we put a bit of chance into the narrative process:

- Use variations in the turn-taking. It doesn't have to be you who decides who's next. It could be the learner who's just finished their turn who names the next one. Alternatively, give each learner a number. When learner number one has narrated for about two minutes, stop them and use an online random number generator to decide who's next. Teens love such a cool element of chance.
- For some more chance elements, hand out cards to your learners before the storytelling session starts. Most of the cards are blank, but a few of them are labelled 'Joker' (a learner who gets this one can nominate someone else to continue the story) and 'Super joker' (this learner can tell you to continue the story instead of them).
- And for yet more chance, add a few cards with a word or a chunk of language written on each of them. Learners who get one of those cards can call out the word/chunk at any time and the narrator has to include it in the story.
- As a variation, ask learners to construe the story in movie terms. You might need to teach some lexis for that, e.g. *director*, *scene*, *flashback*, *flash forward*, *character*. The cards you hand out could be, e.g. *New scene: at a supermarket* (or wherever); *New character* (a hero from the world of sports or film); *Flashback to ...*; *Fast forward to ...*; *Add a bit of magic* (to include a touch of magic realism).

Encourage learners to record their voice

> Current technology offers great opportunities for learners to record themselves. The recordings can be used to increase the amount of listening learners do.

Podcasting can be very motivating for teens, as it may help them find their own 'voice' in English. The internet offers a wide range of free recording devices for video blogging, podcasting and even video lecturing.

Have a discussion about what kind of text learners would most like to record for their classmates. Possible text types range from an inspiring story, to a regular podcast about a topic important to them, to a video lecture. Look for a couple of examples on the web, and play them in class to stimulate ideas. Learners can either make the recordings individually or in pairs (about a topic of mutual interest). Agree the approximate length with them beforehand – depending on the level of the class, five to six minutes works well. It's important, too, that they commit to a deadline – probably about a week's time – when their recording will be available online.

Then learners listen to several of the recordings their classmates have produced. A random pair activity is a good way for learners to give each other feedback. Make sure they do so in a constructive way. Give them some language if needed, e.g. *What I liked about your podcast was ... I really enjoyed what you said about ... What did you find most interesting about your recording?* etc.

It's important that you yourself show an interest in your learners' recordings. Otherwise they might lose interest in them. Ideally, learners comment regularly on each other's recordings on the actual website. Make sure you leave comments, too.

I've noticed that it's better to give learners individual feedback on language. Alternatively, you may offer to look at their notes or script before the recording, or listen to a trial run to help them with pronunciation, stress and intonation.

42 Ways of supporting intensive listening

> Teens can become frustrated by factual texts for intensive
> listening. So they need help in the form of strategies to
> facilitate their listening and give them a sense of achievement.

The classroom is not always the best place to develop intensive listening skills. This is why I regularly give learners listening homework (mini-lectures, interviews with experts, news programmes, etc.). This means they can listen individually, or perhaps with a partner, at their own pace, in an environment that is acoustically better than most classrooms. These days, most coursebooks offer downloadable audio files with recordings of texts to listen to on smartphones or other devices.

Here are some strategies you could show learners to support intensive listening:

- Produce a gapped-out copy of the tapescript. Suggest that learners listen to the whole text first without looking at the handout, and then listen again, filling in the gaps while listening.
- Another time, ask learners to listen to a two-minute (maximum) text and transcribe what they hear. They can stop the audio, rewind it and start again as often as they like.
- If your learners are tech-savvy, tell them to find free software or an app that allows them to slow down an audio without changing the pitch. This can be very helpful in decoding difficult words and sound combinations, especially when used in combination with a(n) (online) dictionary.
- Ask learners to transcribe an audio text and bring their transcription to class. Hand out a copy of the tapescript and ask them to compare it to their own transcription. Tell them to give themselves a score out of 100.
- Another time, divide the class into groups A and B. For homework, ask the learners in group A to listen to one audio, and the learners in B to another. Tell them to write a transcription and translate that into their own language. The next day at school, form A and B pairs and ask them to use the translation as a basis to tell their partner about the text they have listened to.

E: Speaking

With 17 tips, this section is the longest in the book –
justifiably so, I believe, in response to the point made
by many colleagues that it is often so very difficult
to get teens to talk in the target language. There are
sound psychological reasons explaining why the
most talkative teen can all of a sudden turn into a
monosyllabic stony-faced automaton. Changing that
for the better requires the use of a range of strategies
aimed to show our learners both that we take
them seriously – their emotions, fears (of making
mistakes), their opinions, their interests and their
own language – and that we can lead them, with
the help of the right support and inspiring activities,
into a safe and engaged use of the new language.

43 Use substitution tables
44 Engage your learners in small talk
45 Use anecdotes
46 Ask the right questions
47 Deal with silence successfully
48 Do use drills
49 Engage learners in effective roleplay
50 Have five-minute activities ready
51 Encourage learners to speak personally
52 Motivate your learners to stick to English in class
53 Design engaging problem-solving tasks
54 Show me your stickers and I'll tell you ...
55 Use concentric circles to foster fluency
56 Use consensograms as a basis for discussions
57 Engage learners in gallery walk conversations
58 Encourage discussions about values
59 The role of the learners' own language (L1)

43 Use substitution tables

> **Substitution tables can be really helpful, especially for beginners.**

Substitution tables support learners in creating linguistically correct sentences and also help them express themselves meaningfully. However, substitution tables need to go beyond mechanical drills. Paul Nation (2013) says, 'Teachers need to make sure they not only provide opportunities for exact repetition, but that they also provide opportunities for repetition involving generative use. Retrieval involving generative use is one of the most powerful language learning conditions.'

Here is a substitution table for young teens beginning to learn English.

I	use don't use	my	tablet games console smartphone laptop e-reader	to	play games. listen to music. shop. do homework. talk to my friends.

- Write the table on the board to familiarise learners with a key sentence pattern.
- Read out the top sentence in the table, pointing at it word for word. Get learners to repeat the sentence pattern in chorus and individually, then repeat with new sentences.
- Tell learners that you are going to point at an individual word/ phrase in a column that offers more than one option. Point at a learner and ask them to say a sentence, but to replace your word with another word from the column.
- Give learners half a minute to think up sentences that are correct linguistically *and* express what they want to say. Give an example about yourself.
- React primarily to what learners say by showing an interest in it when you respond. If they make any mistakes, correct them discreetly (see also **29** about discreet error correction).

Nation, P. (2013) *What Should Every EFL Teacher Know?* Compass Publishing. Kindle Edition.

Engage your learners in small talk

> Small talk can make a major contribution to the development of learners' conversational skills, and time given to developing it is time well invested.

Linguists and anthropologists have long recognised the importance of 'phatic' language use in all cultures, what we now negatively call 'gossip' or 'small talk'. Using small talk in the teenage language class gives learners plenty of opportunities to use the new language in a natural and non-threatening way.

Small talk is not necessarily a planned – or indeed a plannable! – activity. The most valuable interactions can happen when something arises that is worth chatting about, and you pick up on that and facilitate a conversation. You can support its development by appearing approachable – for example, by not standing in front of the class, but being seated among the learners, thus signalling 'this is not part of the lesson'.

Observe the class, and react to stimuli that come from the learners. Pick up on a learner's non-verbal reaction to something that has been said about the here-and-now, the trivial, the topical, etc. This would include prompts like: *Has anyone been watching that series on TV about …?* etc. Let small talk emerge. This doesn't mean that small talk is necessarily trivial, but that it arises naturally out of the immediate context – or the shared context – of the learners.

Keep your eyes and ears open for things your learners have done well, both in and out of school: playing in the school band, scoring a goal for the school team, helping a friend in trouble, what have you. Acknowledge their achievement aloud, and wait for reactions.

Fine, D. (2014) *Beyond Texting: The Fine Art of Face-to-Face Communication for Teenagers.* Cannon Publishers.

Thornbury, S. (2005) *How to Teach Speaking.* Harlow: Pearson Education Limited.

45 Use anecdotes

> Anecdotes are an indispensable ingredient of human interaction. In class, they create a relaxed atmosphere and foster the natural use of English.

In teenage classes, I have very successfully used anecdotes about myself at my learners' age – my friendships, how I spent my free time, my favourite teachers, my heroes, life lessons that I learned. These kinds of stories are good because you can plan them beforehand.

- Tell your learners an anecdote (it's always better to relate anecdotes spontaneously, rather than reading them out), omitting the ending, and ask them to finish your story from your (first person) perspective. Or encourage them to work out the ending by asking you *Yes/No* questions.
- Show learners an object or picture. Tell them you'd like to relate an anecdote about it, and get them to come up with suggestions for it.
- Tell an anecdote and include an untrue element and get them to identify it. Or tell them three short anecdotes, one of them fabricated, and get them to spot that one.
- Show them the structure of anecdotes: Introduction: *Did I tell you about ...? This reminds me of ...*; Setting the stage: *Who? Where? When?* Development: *First ..., but then ... / Eventually ...*; Conclusion: *This is how I learned ... / When I look back now ...* .
- Show videos of people telling anecdotes well. Elicit important strategies such as eye contact, pausing (to increase tension), intensifiers (*really, so, extremely ...*), active listening (*Wow! I can't believe it!*) and questions (*Were you alone there? Why was that?*), etc.
- Get learners to tell anecdotes in pairs, and give feedback to improve their storytelling. Then they pair up and retell their anecdotes.

Bilbrough, N. (2007) *Dialogue Activities*. Cambridge: Cambridge University Press.

McCarthy, M. (1991) *Discourse Analysis for Language Teachers*. Cambridge: Cambridge University Press.

Thornbury, S. (2005) *How to Teach Speaking*. Harlow: Pearson Education Limited.

Ask the right questions

> In many classrooms, the standard pattern of interaction is
> Question – Answer – Formal Feedback. But this pattern
> is not the best way of developing natural speaking.

Unlike in real life, teachers often ask questions whose answer they already know: *What is the past of 'go'?* Asking 'real' questions in the classroom as well can improve the quality and quantity of learners' conversation, but if you then notice that you're getting short answers to such questions, it could be that learners are not interested in the topic, or your questions are 'closed' – eliciting *Yes/No* answers – or that you're not giving your learners enough thinking time.

Ask open rather than closed questions. That is, instead of going: *Did you see The Revenant? – Yes. – Did you like it? – No.* etc. you could say, e.g. *I saw (title of a film) recently. I'm still not sure what to think of it. What good films have you seen lately? What did you like about them?* These open questions allow you to show your learners that you are seriously interested in the content of what they have to say, and not just in the (correctness of the) language they produce. *What makes an interesting lesson? / Why do you think some lessons are boring and some are not? / If you were a teacher, what would you find easy or difficult about your job?*

Extend the conversational range by linking your question to another topic. Continue with something along the lines of: *... or have you been too busy with school work to watch any good movies recently?* That way you are giving them an alternative topic to investigate.

When you have asked a question, give your learners time to think. You can model this by occasionally saying: *Mmm. Let me think ... .*

47 Deal with silence successfully

Silence is sometimes perceived as awkward, and I've heard teachers say they feel uncomfortable when their class is silent. But the right kind of silence can be a good thing.

One of the most exciting parts of my teacher-training career was sitting in on my trainees' teaching practice. And I often noticed that they found it difficult to deal with silence. Of course, a good language teacher wants their classrooms to vibrate with interaction – but a bit of silence every now and then can be invaluable.

Make time for learners to see you're thinking, and indicate that to them by saying something like: *That's a good point. Let me think about it.* Make sure you keep quiet for three or four seconds before you continue. When you ask a question that none of your learners can answer, invite them to take a bit of time to think.

Then keep an eye on them to pick up body language indicating they want to speak. Nodding your head or smiling is usually perceived as very supportive in such situations. If a silence lasts too long, get your learners to find the answers in pairs rather than individually.

Sometimes, when a learner is getting stuck, you'll need to guess. Gently prompt language but be ready to offer a different prompt if you have guessed wrong. Here's an example from an A2 class:

    A: I no forehead.
    T: Sorry, Anna?
    A: I *no* forehead.
    T: Have you got a headache? (mimes headache) Do you want to drink some water?
    A: No, I no forehead ... erm ... write. (pretends to be writing)
    T: Ah, you don't know how to spell 'forehead'. (goes to board and writes word up)
    A: Thank you.

Do use drills

> For awareness and automatic recall, drills in language learning are as essential as repetition of specific movements in sports training.

Drilling not only helps reinforce useful chunks, but also draws attention to key language items. Here are three informal and interesting ways to introduce drills:

1   **Repetition in dialogue:** starts with a snippet of dialogue, such as:
    A: *How much is the T-shirt? –* B: £6. – A: *Oh, really? That's a bargain.*
    Now get your learners to repeat the dialogue, but with new words in it:

T: jeans	Ls: How much are the jeans?
T: £9.	Ls: Oh, really? That's a bargain.
T: sunglasses	Ls: How much are the sunglasses?
T: £500.	Ls: Oh, really? That's … ridiculous!
	(prompted by the teacher).

    T: shoes, etc.

2   **Backward chaining:** a powerful technique to remember longer utterances, uses rhythm and a fast pace. The target utterance here is:
    I wonder if there is anything else I can do?

T: do	Ls: do
T: can do	Ls: can do
T: else I can do	Ls: else I can do

    T: anything else I can do? etc.

3   **Intonation patterns in chunks of language:** again, using rhythm and a fast pace, add different voice modalities – whispering, shouting, sounding happy/sad, etc. – to support learners' noticing and memory.
    T: Don't get me wrong. – Ls: Don't get me wrong.
    T: I'd rather you asked. – Ls: I'd rather you asked.
    T: Don't get me wrong. I'd rather you asked. – Ls: Don't get me wrong. I'd rather you asked.
    T: I'd rather you asked before using my pen. – Ls: I'd rather you asked before using my pen.
    T: Don't get me wrong. I'd rather you asked before using my pen, etc.

Engage learners in effective roleplay

> Roleplay activities should go beyond acting out language by heart, enabling learners to become more spontaneous and 'own' the language they are using.

When learners act out dialogues from a coursebook, they aren't interacting authentically. Authentic communication requires them to learn to really listen to each other, be flexible in what they say, ask clarifying questions, and rephrase content that has not been understood by their partner.

Ask a learner to act out a scripted dialogue with you. But then, don't just follow their language slavishly; instead, change the dialogue a bit as you go along (by pretending not to have understood, or adding non-scripted content, or asking additional questions, etc.). If necessary, help the learner by whispering to them what they could say back to you.

Gradually encourage learners to make changes to scripted dialogues themselves. Go through the dialogue with them and see if they can make any suggestions as to what could be changed or added. Make sure they understand that it's perfectly OK to make mistakes as they go.

Ask learners to think how the dialogue would be different if, e.g. the age of one of the speakers, or their own age, changed, or if the relationship between the speakers was different. Give them a bit of time to prepare their roleplay together and discuss the outline of the conversation. But tell them never to write up their roleplays beforehand. Reading a piece of text aloud is a very different skill, and it doesn't prepare learners to speak naturally.

Teenagers are often quite keen on acting out roleplays based on narratives they have read or listened to. You could encourage them to act out a different ending to the story, or add a surprise element to a scene from the story, etc. In each of these cases, give them just one or two minutes to discuss the outline of their roleplay, and then act it out straight away.

A short speaking activity can raise the learners' energy level, bring about a welcome change or meaningfully fill a gap at the end of a lesson.

Here are some of the five-minute activities I use a lot:

- Display a provocative or funny picture/cartoon. Give the learners a bit of time, and – if necessary – a few prompts: *This picture (cartoon) reminds me of … / It makes me wonder if … / I (don't) find it … .* Get learners to talk in pairs or small groups.

- Write statements, half of them true, half false, on slips of paper, one for each learner, and hand them out. Tell them some statements are false. Get learners to walk around for two minutes, asking other learners for their opinion about their statement. Then ask the learners to form their own opinions and share them with the class, giving their reasons.

- Write questions on slips of paper. Put each question in a balloon and inflate it. Form groups of three to five learners. Give each a balloon. Ask them to pop it and discuss their question: a fun activity that kindles learners' curiosity!

- Write a quotation on the board, but leave out a word or a phrase, e.g. *I wanna be the _____ _____ brother, not his _____* (Martin Luther King). Ask learners to work in small groups and try to complete the quotation. (Key: white / man's / brother-in-law).

- Ask learners to pair up and decide who's A and who's B. Then tell them that As are optimists, Bs pessimists. Give them a statement, e.g. *In a few years' time, robots will do most of the manual work currently done by humans.* Get them to react from their A or B perspective.

You can find a whole range of short activities in the reference below.

Ur, P. and Wright, A. (1994) *Five-Minute Activities: A Resource Book of Short Activities.* Cambridge: Cambridge University Press.

Encourage learners to speak personally

> The more we can get teens to express their own thoughts, emotions and beliefs, the more relevant the language-learning process will become for them.

There's a belief that teenagers hate personalisation. But in fact, much depends on whether we can manage to arouse their interest, help them feel safe and respected, and show them we enjoy being with them.

There are a few ground rules to make personalisation work effectively:

1 Never push learners to reveal more than they want; tell them to 'pass' on a question they feel is too personal;
2 Give learners the option of choosing what they want to talk about; *and*
3 Arrange activities that allow learners to speak out of the public eye. Milling-around is especially good for that; as everyone is talking at the same time, it's hard to hear what others are saying.

Here are some examples of personalisation activities that work well:

- The Star Warmer: learners draw a five-pointed star. On its points they write: the name of a person important to them, a date, a number, a place and a symbol (emoji, logo, etc.). They then stand up or move into small groups, and show their star. Model the questions that they can ask each other with an example: *Is she your sister? Is that the day you moved to …?*
- Dictate six sentences about yourself, two of them made up. Get learners to talk in pairs and detect the two. Then ask them to write six similar sentences about themselves, and work in small groups.
- In another lesson dictate some more sentences about yourself. Ask learners to change them so that they are true for themselves. Then, in small groups, they ask the other group members to guess what they have written about themselves.

Motivate your learners to stick to English in class

> It's not always easy to get learners to use English, especially in pair or group work. It pays to tackle this issue systematically.

Especially in adolescence, teens gain security from their peer group, and feel it's vital not to 'stick out'. Hence, they want to look and talk like their peers, and won't easily do what their teacher suggests if it's different. This is especially so when the 'group barometers' – learners with strong personalities who are admired or feared by others – think talking English in class is uncool.

One reason why some learners are reluctant to use English in class is that they're worried about making mistakes. But don't let them use their own language as the main means of communication, and be persistent in using English yourself. That said, have a chat with your learners – if necessary, in their own language – and elicit, and write on the board, reasons why it's a good idea to talk English in class (see **59**).

Have learners brainstorm what stops them from using English. You'll probably get suggestions such as: *I don't know English well enough. / I'm too shy.* etc. Write their points on the board. Point out that in real life people frequently have to communicate with others in a language they don't speak very well. Elicit from them that in those situations, accuracy is far less important than getting your message across somehow, no matter how many mistakes you make.

Head a poster 'Our record for speaking English'. Use your phone stopwatch to check how long learners manage to stick to English. Write it on the poster. If you do this regularly, you'll notice that learners get quite eager to break their own record, and will gradually use English more readily.

What's essential is that you a) praise learners for their efforts, and b) are *always* non-judgemental about their errors. If you really need to correct something, it's crucial to do this discreetly (see **29** for suggestions on error correction).

53 Design engaging problem-solving tasks

> Problem-solving tasks are meaning-focused and hence very important for the development of learners' speaking skills.

But if we want learners to take the tasks seriously and be fully engaged in them, the design of problem-solving tasks is crucial. Paul Nation (2013) emphasises the need to design problem-solving activities with three parameters in mind: outcome, useful procedures and challenge.

- **Outcome:** tasks that are too open, e.g. *What can our town do for young people?*, are not well designed. A much more focused discussion will take place if you present a problem by asking learners to make concrete suggestions for a desired outcome, e.g. *In a recent survey, 70% of all teenagers in our town said that life in this town is boring. Give three suggestions to make this town more interesting for teens.*
- **Useful procedures:** formats with two or three steps require learners to think more carefully and hence produce more language. Adding choices, and asking them to rank-order them, engages their critical thinking. A progression – *individual – pairs – small groups – whole class* will give them more speaking opportunities. So you could follow up the initial task presented above with, e.g. *Compare your ideas in small groups and choose what you think are the six best suggestions. Give reasons. Rank-order the group's ideas and present them to the whole class.*
- **Challenge:** adding a challenge, as in the task below, will help the learners be more creative and think outside the box, leading to different views and suggestions. Prompt learners to give reasons for their suggestions or choices wherever possible.

Task: *The mayor of your town wants to make sure teens spend less time in shopping malls and on the streets. Suggest how to refurbish your school so learners would want to spend some of their free time there.*

Challenge: *The city council hasn't got the money to finance any expensive ideas. So the school would need to raise the money.*

Nation, P. (2013) *What Should Every EFL Teacher Know?* Compass Publishing. Kindle Edition.

Show me your stickers and I'll tell you ...

(Bumper) stickers are popular with people of all ages and walks of life. Teens often find them cool if everyone else – or the most popular learners, at least – approves of them.

Teenagers love T-shirts or stickers with messages in English on them. Sometimes they find them cool because of what the slogan says, but sometimes they haven't understood the message. This can become the topic of a series of conversations.

- Show learners a photo or a copy of a sticker or slogan on a T-shirt, e.g. *Want to meet God? Keep texting while you drive.* Ask them to explain what this message means and where they think it is from.
- Tell learners to say who they think would wear a T-shirt or have a bumper sticker on their car with this message on it. Help them with language if needed, e.g.
  I think the person who'd put this slogan up is maybe still a child / fairly young / middle-aged / retired because ...
  As far as the lifestyle of this person is concerned, I think they have got / own / live in / play / listen to ...
  This person's political views are probably rather conservative. / a bit radical. / not very different from most people's.
- Ask the class to work in pairs and imagine that the person who put up this sticker/is wearing a T-shirt with this slogan is having an argument (jokingly or seriously) with someone about the message of the slogan. Give learners two or three minutes to prepare the dialogue – but they shouldn't write it down or even take notes.
- Learners act out their dialogue.
- Invite the class to bring in their own slogans. Repeat the activity in another lesson based on the stickers/slogans the learners have brought to class.

55 Use concentric circles to foster fluency

> Concentric circles are ideal for fluency practice, increase learners' talking time and give them opportunities to learn from each other.

This speaking activity needs two circles of learners, with the learners standing in the inner circle facing those in the outer one. In classrooms with little open space, the learners in the outer circle could stand with their backs to the classroom walls.

- Tell learners to form the concentric circles. Explain to them that you'll give them a topic, e.g. *Compare your route to school*, to talk about for a minute. Ask them to make sure this is a two-way chat and not a monologue. Tell them that when you clap your hands, it'll be time to stop their conversation; the learners standing in the outer circle should move anti-clockwise, to face a new partner, while the learners in the inner circle stay where they are. They should then say hello to their new partner and wait for your next instruction.
- Give learners a minute or so for their chat, then clap your hands.
- When learners have moved and said hello, tell them to talk about the same topic with their new partner. Tell them that they can use language and ideas they heard from their previous partner. Tell them that they will get another chance to talk about the same topic to their next partner, to enrich what they want to say.
- Then after the *third* round give learners a new topic to talk about, and tell them they'll get a chance to have a chat about it three times again.
- In future lessons, make sure you get learners to talk about each topic twice. Add a few new topics, too. In another lesson, ask them to talk about each of the initial topics to one partner, and to two more partners about the topics added in the previous lesson.
- Gradually increase the time you allow for each chat, and ask learners to suggest topics for the chats.

> To increase teens' level of engagement and enhance their thinking, engage them in cognitively challenging tasks.

Teenage learners love being challenged with thought-provoking questions, but, like most of us, they need time to think before they feel comfortable sharing their thoughts with a bigger group. The consensogram gives learners a safe space to think and helps them compare their ideas between themselves before they share with the whole class.

To set up a consensogram, follow these steps:

- Hand out a number of thought-provoking statements, e.g. *Top car racers deserve every cent they earn. / Drugs will never be an issue in car racing.*

- Ask learners to take a minute to think about each statement and write their agreement with each one on a scale of 1 to 6 (1 = completely disagree / 6 = totally agree), then write one or two sentences about each statement to justify their choice.

- Draw a chart for each statement on a large sheet of poster paper and put them up. Learners draw dots or stick labels onto them, to indicate their level of agreement:

1	2	3	4	5	6
● ● ●	● ● ●	● ● ● ●	●	● ●	● ● ● ●

- Ask learners to form small groups to discuss the outcomes of the survey, and give their own opinions. Get them to form new groups at least twice.
- Round this off with a whole-group discussion of the survey.

For an analysis of a range of activities fostering active engagement in critical thinking, see the reference below.

Stobaugh, R. R. and Love, S. L. *Fusing Critical Thinking with Kinesthetic Learning.* Available at: https://www.mentoringminds.com/learn/white-papers/fusing-critical-thinking-kinesthetic-learning/

57 Engage learners in gallery walk conversations

> This activity invites learners to exchange ideas while moving around the classroom.

When you invite teens to walk round the classroom thoughtfully, reacting to stimuli on the walls, and share their thoughts, they will feel taken more seriously, and will therefore more readily use the target language. This is how it works:

- Find some thought-provoking questions suitable for your learners' age and language level. They could be philosophical (like the ones below, which I've used with B2 learners), or scientific, or aimed at leading into a forthcoming coursebook topic, or used for revision.
  - What does it mean to live a good life?
  - If you could teach every adult in the world one concept, what would that be?
  - Is the meaning of life the same for animals and humans?
  - What is the purpose of art?
  - Who has more freedom – animals or humans?
  - What is the relationship between intelligence and happiness?

- Write each question on a poster-size piece of paper. Put them on the walls.
- Divide the class into groups of three to five learners. Assign a 'home poster' to each group. Give each group a felt tip pen in a distinctive colour, and nominate one learner as the group recorder. Tell them that they'll have three to five minutes to discuss the question as a team. The recorder writes their thoughts (legibly!) on the poster, leaving space for others' comments.
- Ask each group to move on to another poster. Another learner in each group becomes the recorder. Give them three to five minutes to react to the new question and comment on the ideas added by the previous group.
- When all the groups have worked on all the posters, each group goes back to their home poster. Give them eight to ten minutes to synthesise the ideas on their poster, and prepare a group presentation for the whole class.

Encourage discussions about values

> **Values are about what is morally right or wrong. They cannot be taught directly.**

Values are handed down to the next generation through the behaviour young people observe in relevant others. This is why your own behaviour is so important; if you want your learners to become empathetic listeners, the way you model empathetic listening is crucial.

Learners pick up values, too, from the narratives they hear – from their peers, relevant others, movies and books. And there is a third way, as in the example below: getting learners to explore values by exchanging their views about them. The psychologist Jay Giedd emphasises that the plasticity of the teenage brain is enormous and that conversations with teens about real-life topics, such as *freedoms* and *responsibilities*, can have a positive influence on their development. 'Freedoms' and 'responsibilities' are, of course, examples of values. (If you are interested in Jay Giedd's work, see the reference below.) This is one way you can address values with your class:

- Present to your learners a set of 'value statements', e.g.
  - To be successful in life, you need 1% inspiration and 99% perspiration. (Edison)
  - Laughter is the best medicine.
  - It's in times of trouble that you find out who your friends are.
  - If you feel bad all the time when you're with someone, you should stop seeing them.
- Get learners to look at the statements. Ask them to do a PM activity for each statement – that is, to find **Plus/Minus** arguments. For the first statement, e.g. **P:** *I know somebody who is an extremely successful businesswoman. She is very hard-working.* **M:** *Some people have never worked hard in their life – they're just lucky. And many hard-working people are never successful.*
- Ask learners to share their views with a partner, and follow this up with a whole-class discussion.

Giedd, J. (2015) *The Amazing Teen Brain*. Scientific American.

The role of the learners' own language (L1)

> It is not advisable to completely exclude the use of the learners' L1.

Philip Kerr argues that all learning is based on prior knowledge, so our learners' L1 is an important foundation that should not be ignored. In fact, most authorities in ELT have maintained for some time that the principled use of the learners' own language can be important for language learning. But teachers are often unsure about its role. Let's look at a few examples of how L1 can be used in a principled way:

- With low-level learners, when learners don't understand an instruction, use the sandwich technique: say it in English, then the same in their L1, and in English again. This gives learners security, and they will rapidly develop a good comprehension of such instructions. Then stop the translating!
- With learners of all levels you can use 'mediation' activities. After, e.g. listening to a song in English, say: *Imagine listening to this song with a friend who doesn't speak English. Explain to them in your own language what the song is about.* This is great to do as a roleplay!
- Learners read a text, then run it through an online translator and print it. In pairs, they improve the online translation (using, e.g. their phones to access online dictionaries). This activity usually gets learners to think about their L1 and their L2.
- Collect typical mistakes caused by the learners' L1. Write them on the board and ask learners to correct them. Have them translate both the correct and the incorrect ones into their L1 and compare them.
- Do the same with difficult grammar structures, especially those that are conceptually different from the learners' L1.

You can find an insightful discussion of the use of the learners' L1 in ELT and lots of practical activities in the reference below.

Kerr, P. (2014) *Translation and Own-language Activities*. Cambridge: Cambridge University Press.

F: Reading

Reading requires effort and passion, and to some teenagers it may not seem like something they want to work at. After all, there is a world of electronic temptations out there that require far less effort and feel as though they are going to be a lot more entertaining. Yet many teens are concerned about their future, and how successful they will be in tomorrow's world. So this section provides a range of ideas: some that support less motivated readers; some that give a fascinating insight into what happens in the brain when we read and some that provide clear guidelines to help develop the reading skills needed for passing exams.

Create awareness of what's happening while reading

> Helping learners become aware of what's happening inside their heads when they read can improve their reading, and increase their enjoyment of it.

When we read a novel, for example, we constantly want to find out what happens next. A little experiment helps learners explore what's going on in their minds when they read:

- Select a very short story, preferably ending in a single sentence containing a twist or a surprise. Tell learners that you are going to present a text to them in a very unusual way: sentence by sentence, with a pause of about 10 seconds after each sentence.
- Ask learners to remain silent during each pause in order to write down what they expect will come next.
- Carry on until you get to the pause just before the last sentence (which you're not going to tell them – yet).
- Tell learners to discuss these questions in pairs or small groups: *At each pause, what did you expect to happen next? And what are your expectations for the ending of the story?*
- Discuss the relevance of learners' experiences to their reading in general. Suggest that a pattern of *pausing – thinking what you've read – becoming aware of your expectations* could be a useful strategy for them to enrich their own reading.

See Appendix 1 for a story whose first paragraph I have used successfully with young adult A2 learners. It's the introduction to a text about Jonnie Peacock, the gold winner of the 100m race at the 2010 Paralympics in London, and is a slight adaptation of a text from Doff et al. (see reference below).

Doff, A., Thaine, C., Puchta, H., Stranks, J. and Lewis-Jones, P. (2015) *Empower. Elementary Student's Book*. Cambridge: Cambridge University Press.

Vary the lead-in activities you use

> When we read in real life, we choose what we read, but in
> the classroom the learners usually have no choice.

So in order to avoid learners reading the text 'cold', we could involve
them in meaningful lead-in activities. These I believe need to accord
with three key criteria:

1   activation of the learners' prior knowledge (usually done through
    some sort of brainstorming);
2   development of the learners' predictions of what they are about to
    read; *and*
3   arousal of their curiosity in the text/topic.

Here are ideas I have successfully used:

- Write four to six keywords or a sentence on the board and make
  sure learners understand the meaning. Get them to call out words
  and phrases that come to mind in connection with the words/
  sentence. Write these associations on the board too. Then ask
  learners to predict what the text will be about.
- If you are working with a coursebook, ask learners to slip a pencil
  into it at the text they are going to read and shut the book. Tell them
  that on your signal they are going to open the book again and in
  ten seconds try to understand as much as possible about the text on
  that page; they should look at the title, the pictures and the layout of
  the text, and skim read as much as they can. Tell them to shut their
  book and call out words and phrases for you to write on the board.
  Continue as suggested in the bullet point above.
- Bring some realia or images to class that are related in some way
  to the topic or text. Wait for learners to react and elicit their
  associations and expectations. (I have, for example, successfully put
  a bottle of dirty water on the teacher's desk as an introduction to
  a text about the pollution of our water.) Make sure you elicit your
  learners' own thoughts – and don't lecture them!

62 Use motivating tasks in connection with extensive reading

> Boring activities can kill joy in extensive reading, so use motivating tasks in connection with longer texts.

Whether you use graded readers, young adult novels (they are usually easy to read) or 'real' books will depend on your learners' language level and how eager they are to read.

Use some pre-reading activities to arouse your learners' interest in the text and activate their pre-knowledge (see also **61**):

- Cover the title on the cover and ask your learners to come up with a snappy one, or show illustrations from the book and ask learners to come up with a storyline.
- Present all the chapter titles. Encourage learners to come up with a storyline. Or give each learner the title of a chapter and ask them to stand up, confer with each other and arrange themselves in the correct sequence.
- Give learners some keywords from Chapter 1 and let them speculate on the type of book, its storyline and characters.
- Use while-reading activities to help the less experienced readers catch up with things they might not have understood. Ask learners to collect good sayings/interesting sentences, etc. from the book on a poster while they are reading. Put the quotes into speech bubbles.
- After the learners have read Chapter 1, ask them to continue the story.

Post-reading activities are often more engaging when they involve the learners more deeply in the story and engage them creatively:

- Ask a learner to talk for a minute about the book they have read in order to 'sell' it to somebody who hasn't read it.
- The (main) characters from the book give a press conference. Some learners play the parts of the characters, others the journalists.

I learned most of these activities from the reference below.

Holzmann, C. (2014) *101 Young Adult Novels for Your English Language Class*. Helbling.

Help learners become fluent readers

> Fluency is important in reading – if it takes a learner a lot of time to decode each individual word, their overall comprehension gets blocked.

So we need to make sure learners get lots of practice in reading fluency. Skilled readers move their eyes smoothly from left to right (in a language like English). They often take in whole phrases and not just individual words, so they can retain what they are reading and comprehend it more easily. It's important for learners to realise that fluency is an important reading skill, and you can help them understand this:

- Select a short paragraph from a reading text, and set up a presentation that reveals the text one word at a time. Then set up another, using a similar text, with three to five words at a time. Make sure the print is big enough for everyone in the class to read it.
- In class, tell your learners you will present a text to them in an unusual way – word by word – and ask them to remember as much of it as they can. Reveal the words about every two seconds. Then show the second text, revealing the chunks at the same pace.
- Then ask learners to talk about the experience and to summarise what they have read. Chances are pretty high that learners will comment it was much easier for them to make sense of the second presentation.
- Ask your learners to keep this in mind when they read – i.e. they should try and take in groups of words that are meaningful, rather than just individual words.
- Every now and again, ask your learners to find short texts online as homework, then in class read them and share what they have read in pair or group work.

64 Use interactive reading ideas

> **Learners who are not keen readers in their mother tongue frequently see reading as boring.**

One way of changing learners' attitude towards reading is to do it on the move.

- Hand out a short text. Ask learners to walk around the classroom without looking at their texts. Tell them that they should talk to another learner for about 20 seconds, discussing what they expect the text to be about. Then tell them they should stop and read their own text for just 20 seconds, then move on to another learner, to share the information they have got out of the text so far. Repeat for another three or four rounds of reading and sharing – 20 seconds each time.
- Prepare copies of short texts, one per learner, of a particular genre, e.g. human-interest stories from newspapers (clippings from sports magazines, short narratives, etc.). Stick the texts on the classroom walls, with plenty of space around each one. Place a block of sticky labels near each of the texts and ask learners to grab a pen and walk round the classroom. Tell them that on your signal they should read a text and write their comments on a label that they then stick up next to the text. Afterwards, walk from text to text and discuss the learners' comments.
- Do a 'reading race'. Choose a text full of information – maybe a page from a free newspaper, prepare questions about the text and write these on strips of card, numbered on the back. In class, place the cards, numbers up, on a table at the front. Distribute a copy of the text to different groups. One member of each group takes a question from the table and returns with it to their group, who looks for the answer in their text and writes it on a sheet of paper, numbering the answer. The question is then returned to the table, and another chosen. They continue until they have answered all the questions. The first group to answer all the questions correctly is the winner.

When learners do a listening task, they are unlikely to read the audio script at the same time. However, if they do this occasionally, it can be of great help to them.

Apps that show the lyrics while playing songs are popular with teens, as understanding song lyrics is difficult. Short words, such as *of*, *to* and *for*, can be difficult to hear. Likewise, certain letters that we hear when words are spoken in isolation seem to disappear in connected speech. In *We asked Tom*, for example, we can't hear /k/ or /d/.

In order to facilitate the comprehension of consonant–consonant word juncture, my co-author of a number of coursebook projects, Jeff Stranks, recommends asking learners to go through a paragraph of a text they have read and mark all the words that end in a *t* or *d*, for example:

It was the semi-final of the 400 metres. The crowd were ready for a great race. The British athlete Derek Redmond was one of the favourites. At first, he was running well. Then, after about 150 metres, he felt a pain in his leg. He fell down with a bad injury and …

Play the recording of the piece and ask learners to pay attention to the sounds they have marked. They will find that *t* or *d* at the end of a word is pronounced when followed by a vowel, but not when followed by another consonant. Matching what learners *hear* with what they *see* has lots of positive effects in terms of matching sound and spelling, and coping with ellipsis.

Another idea is that after you have used a listening text for comprehension tasks, play the text again and let learners read as they listen. This could be extended to an activity where they mark up the text, e.g. identifying tone groups, stressed words, etc., then read it aloud in pairs.

Puchta, H., Stranks, J. and Lewis-Jones, P. (2015) *Think Student's Book 1*. Cambridge: Cambridge University Press.

66 Regularly revisit texts learners have read

> When learners have finished reading a text, it pays *not* to see it as 'done and dusted'. Texts are treasure troves of language, so they are worth revisiting regularly.

Go back to texts your learners have read, so they can dig out important language, such as collocations, lexical sets, formulaic expressions, discourse markers, etc. The more often you do this, the better.

Collocations: these are tricky because there are no rules governing them, and learners need to remember verbatim that it's, e.g. *do* (not ~~make~~) *your homework*, *make* (not ~~do~~) *an effort* and *take* (not ~~make~~) *a break*. Other collocations such as binominal expressions demand the correct word order: *black and white* (not ~~white and black~~), *peace and quiet*, etc.

- Give learners copies of a paragraph from a text they have read where you have deleted parts of collocations. They reconstruct the collocations in pairs and then check them in the text.

Chunks of language: many modern coursebooks offer conversations featuring high-frequency chunks – *Nice one. / I didn't mean to ...*, etc. (For more on chunks of language, see the reference below.)

- Write up on the board in a jumbled order a list of the phrases your learners have come across in a conversation in the text. In pairs, learners number the phrases in the order of their appearance in the text. Then ask them to go back to the conversation and check.
- Learners work in pairs and test each other on the phrases: one learner says a word from one of the phrases, and the other learner responds by completing the phrase. Then swap.

Interleaved grammar drills: challenge your learners by getting them to drill grammar structures previously learned with content from a text read recently – a fun activity that requires creativity and language precision at the same time.

- Say, e.g. *Create 2nd conditional clauses with content from text X. Or: How many passive sentences can you make using text Y?* etc.

Thornbury, S. (2019) available at: https://www.cambridge.org/elt/blog/2019/11/01/chunk-spotting-users-guide/

> The more vividly learners activate all their senses while reading a narrative, the more they will get out of it and the better they will remember it.

The following activity has been developed based on an idea I learned from Mario Rinvolucri. It fosters learners' ability to develop their sensory awareness while reading a text. It can be used, too, to teach specific lexis that learners need in order to talk about different sensory qualities. The activity aims at getting learners to do an in-depth exploration of a story by identifying with one of the protagonists and trying to see what's going on through the protagonist's eyes, to hear what the protagonist hears, and feel, smell and taste whatever they imagine the person they are identifying with would feel, smell or taste at various stages of the narrative. Depending on the level of the class, you may want to brainstorm adjectives, nouns, verbs and fixed phrases that your learners already know in connection with the five senses, and gradually widen the lexical sets in each of the areas.

- Select a story whose level would be suitable to your learners (or two stories, so half of the class can read story A and the other half story B). Ask them to quickly read through it with the questions *Where? What?* and *Who?* in mind.
- Get learners to imagine they are one of the characters in the story. Invite them to go through the story again and relive the key situations as if they were the character they have chosen, focusing on the sensory perceptions of the character they are identifying with, to explore the story more deeply. Give an example for one sensory area, e.g. *What do I see in this situation? What colours? What shapes?* Give them these prompts to structure their sensations:
  I tried to identify with (name).
  I could see/hear/feel/taste/smell (noun).
  It looked/sounded/felt/tasted/smelled (*like* + noun) *or* (adjective).

> Intensive reading requires focus and practice. When
> learners have read a text, we need to make sure we first
> check their comprehension.

Intensive reading relates to more challenging, usually shorter, texts than
those used for extensive reading. Intensive reading is usually done in
class. Here are a few tips on how to get learners to focus on extracting
meaning, then gradually move on to the analysis of the language in
the text:

- Ask, e.g. three overall comprehension questions, three questions
  about details in the text and finally three questions about inferencing
  meaning. The latter should be about ideas that are *not* directly
  expressed in the text; they could be about the meaning of a line, a
  paragraph or the whole text. Inferencing questions often include
  wording such as: *What does the writer suggest ... when he/she
  says ...? Could paragraph X be interpreted to mean ...? Give your
  reasons. / What is the author's view about ...? Quote from the text
  to support your view.*
- Individually, learners circle five words (could be ten depending on
  text length) they want to know the meaning of; they then compare
  notes in pairs, and agree on a shared list; they do this in groups of
  four, then eight, then sixteen, etc. until the whole class has come to a
  consensus. You give the meaning of the words, or allow learners to
  look them up.
- Ask learners how they would say certain structures in their own
  language. Give them a dictogloss activity of a short piece or a
  paragraph of the text (see **77**).
- In addition to the above, give learners a task (or three tasks to
  choose one from) that requires creativity: changing parts of a text,
  rewriting it from a different perspective, adding a paragraph to
  the text, changing the register, writing a reply to it (if it poses a
  question), etc.

> The more skilled your learners' reading, the more they will
> enjoy finding more refined nuances of meaning.

When our learners engage in intensive reading in their L1, their focus is
on extracting the information in the text. On the whole, we can assume
that the skills needed for intensive reading in their L2 are transferable
from their own language, as long as learners are literate in their L1, and
familiar with the text type, the lexis, the grammar and the topic (which
can compensate for gaps in their linguistic knowledge). To scaffold
comprehension, engage learners in predicting its content (from graphic
information, for example, see **61**), ask comprehension questions, ask
more detailed questions, and even elicit translations.

Once learners understand the text, you can focus on analysing its
linguistic features, such as: the macrostructure of the text; the way it is
made cohesive (by linking devices, pronoun reference, etc.); the semantic
chains running through it (e.g. words of the same lexical set); the
consistency of tenses and/or changes in tense; the transitivity patterns
(e.g. use of active v passive), etc.

Announce beforehand that you will set a reading task in each of, say,
ten consecutive lessons. Each text should be more or less the same
length. Before learners read it, hand out a task sheet focusing on one of
the aspects listed above, such as:

- Text type: What kind of text is this? Where would you find this kind
  of a text? What do we know about the author? Who has this text
  been written for?
- Structure: How is the text organised? What is the topic? What are
  the supporting details? What headline would you suggest for each of
  the paragraphs?
- Cohesion: What or who do the following pronouns/adverbials
  (give their specific locations in the text) refer to? How do these
  conjunctions (give their specific locations in the text) influence the
  meaning of the text?

70 Scaffold learners' inferencing skills with the help of poetry

> Inferencing – or 'reading between the lines' – demands a set of skills that requires thorough training.

Quite a few of the teenagers I have worked with have found it difficult to read between the lines, sometimes even in their L1. To develop their inferencing skills, we need to help them get themselves into the writer's head, so they can either:

1 infer the writer's intention/attitude (e.g. is the writer trying to persuade me to buy something?), or

2 infer information that is not explicit because the writer a) is trying to conceal it, or b) sees it as shared knowledge, or c) wants to allow multiple interpretations, as in some poetry.

It's not always easy to guess what it is the writer is *not* saying, but there can be clues that point to the writer's intention/attitude, e.g. evaluative adjectives (*fabulous*, *awesome*, etc.) as in persuasive writing, or the definite article (*Don't forget to feed the cat!*) that indicates shared knowledge.

To scaffold the learners' inferencing skills, use short poems, e.g.

The fireplace is cold, covered with thick ashes.
Again the single light has gone out.
Loneliness, and the night is only half over.
Silence – all I can hear is the voice of a distant mountain stream.

Remind the learners that to answer the questions they will need to read the poem, or parts of it, several times. They may find, too, that not all the questions are equally relevant for all poems.

1 What does the writer see/hear, etc.? Where is the writer?
2 What or who do the personal pronouns refer to?
3 What shared knowledge do words like 'the', 'here/there' refer to?
4 What places or people do the proper nouns refer to?
5 What is the writer's mood?

Stevens, J. (trans.) (1977) *One Robe, One Bowl: The Zen Poetry of Ryōkan.* New York: Weatherhill.

> When learners have read a factual text, ask them to
> analyse the way the information is organised.

Research has shown that creating a concept map has a significantly positive effect on learners' understanding of what they have read, and will result in a higher level of retention than a traditional comprehension task.

Concept maps are visual organisers of information. They are hierarchically structured, and are often tree diagrams. You may initially want to create a concept map together with your learners based on a text they have read. Later, learners can create their own, individually or in pairs or small groups.

- Get learners to identify the main idea of the text and write that at the bottom of the concept tree.
- Then ask them to identify the associated sub-concepts, and write words or phrases on the branches to illustrate the relationships between the ideas. Depending on their age and the complexity of a text, learners should identify between 10 and 20 topics in it.
- Show learners how concept maps can be used later on as a technique to remind themselves of what they have read.
- Demonstrate that they can expand a concept map by, e.g. doing research on ideas in the map and adding what they have found out.
- Say that concept maps can be helpful in preparing a presentation.

Depending on the technology available to your learners, you may want them to use digital concept mapping tools so their maps can easily be shared, co-edited and stored.

Hattie, J. (2012) *Visible Learning for Teachers: Maximising Impact on Learning.* Routledge.

Redford, J., Thiede. K.W., Wiley, J. and Griffin, T. (2012) *Concept Mapping Improves Metacomprehension Accuracy Among 7th Graders.* Boise State University. Scholar Works. Available at: https://scholarworks.boisestate.edu/cgi/viewcontent. cgi?article=1093&context=cifs_facpubs

Read texts out loud

It is not a good idea to practise reading by asking learners to read a text from, e.g. their coursebook, aloud. But certain texts can be appropriate for this purpose, and very helpful.

Michael West (1955) promoted the idea of read-and-look-up: 'The pupils should be made to *look up* when they read aloud. The teacher says, "Don't read to the book! Read to me. Look up at me." He makes them read a phrase or short sentence silently then, *looking up*, say it to someone – to the teacher, or to another pupil, or to the class. Of course, the pupils need to have studied the passage beforehand, so that it is already familiar; and it takes a little time – four or five lessons – to train a class to do this.'

So, what can we do? Here are a few ideas that I have used successfully with my teenage classes:

- Ask your learners to watch a video of some news in English and transcribe a 20–30-second passage from it, word for word. Ideally, this will be done in a computer lab where learners can go online and each student can work on a different piece of news. Encourage them to listen again and again, and to ask another learner or you for help when they get stuck. Get them to practise reading the short text out loud as explained above.
- Ask learners to write a short news story about something that happened to them or somebody they know, in the style of a news report. Help them correct their language, and ask them to practise reading their news story out to their classmates while looking at them (see above).
- Texts written by learners (as, e.g. homework) are ideal for reading out to the class.

West, M. (1955) *Learning to read a foreign language*. London: Longmans, Green.

G: Writing

Learners who can express themselves effectively in writing in a new language often have a clear sense of ownership of it. But in many teenage classrooms, this is an idea that has yet to be explored, especially when writing is seen merely as a way of taking notes for exam preparation, or as a way of practising a new language in the form of grammar activities and drills. So this section focuses on some swift and practical ways of getting learners to write short functional texts, then suggests various ways of involving learners in fun and poetic writing tasks, and rounds off with ideas on how to use 'mentor sentences': literary models of excellence aimed at enriching the learners' own writing styles.

73 Involve learners in writing short texts

> Writing can be frustrating for beginners and for those who are struggling. So teaching them how to write short, meaningful texts can give learners a terrific sense of achievement.

Teenagers should be taught right from the start to write short texts with a communicative purpose:

- **Short emails:** Emails are easy to write. They can be short and informal. Write emails to ask your learners simple questions that they answer as homework. Teach them to send you emails, too.
- **Writing memos:** Show learners what the format of a memo looks like (*To: / From: / Date: / Subject:*). Show learners how to write memos to each other, e.g. when doing a group project.
- **Writing a personal note:** Write short messages to your learners to congratulate them on an achievement, to thank them for something, etc. Encourage them to write notes to each other, too.

Higher-level learners need to practise writing shorter texts, too – in their work life they will be expected to write concisely and clearly.

- Teach learners how to write **customer feedback messages** after buying something online or eating at a restaurant. A text they can publish immediately!
  - Show learners examples of customer feedback messages – for example, on restaurants' homepages or websites for travellers.
  - Analyse their generic structure: greeting / reason for writing / description of problem(s) or reason(s) for praise/criticism.
  - Identify words/expressions used for positive/negative evaluation.
- Hand out a copy of an unnecessarily long email. Tell learners to shorten it so readers will quickly understand it.
- Set up a closed social media group for the class. Encourage learners to chat in English with each other, and with you, too.

Chong, C. S. (2018) 'Where are the short messages in ELT?' *English Teaching Professional.* Available at: https://www.etprofessional.com/where-are-the-short-messages-in-elt

Help learners get into a writing flow

> Successful writers often experience a sense of getting into a writing flow. Some of your learners may need help with that to overcome inhibitions.

Some learners 'think too much'. They may not be able to start because they want to write a particularly good first sentence, and then end up procrastinating, displeased with whatever first sentence comes to mind. Or they may be scared of making too many mistakes and end up blocking themselves rather than getting into the flow of writing.

In order to help learners overcome such blocks, I've found it useful to engage them in very short writing activities. Once learners get used to these, they often comment that they are surprised how much they are able to write in a short period of time.

- Tell learners that we all have an 'inner watchdog' – a nagging and critical voice that we hear in our head sometimes. Tell them that that beast might say things like: *You'll never be able to write an inspiring story. Your grammar just isn't good enough*, etc. Ask them to call out more examples of their own inner watchdogs' voices.
- Ask learners to imagine what writing would be like if they sent their watchdogs out of the classroom for a while.
- Ask learners to write for five minutes as fast as they can without stopping. Tell them that if a thought interrupts their flow, they should not stop writing – rather, they should write that thought down, too. It doesn't matter what they write, nor how well-crafted their sentences are, as nobody (least of all you, the teacher!) will read their texts. Write '5 minutes' on the board, and change the number as the minutes tick down.
- Repeat the exercise regularly and use it for different purposes, for example, at the beginning of the lesson (to explore learners' expectations or their prior knowledge of a topic or theme), or at the end (writing down what their perception of the lesson was), or use a picture or a word or a question as a stimulus.

> When learners transform a text, they have to think deeply about certain aspects of it, and draw on their critical thinking, their general knowledge and their imagination.

There are lots of ways you can get your learners involved in text transformations, which are a good way of helping learners use and re-use language from different perspectives. That gives them the security of being able to recycle language that is already in mind, and create a product that is new.

- Ask your learners to change the text type. Select a short news item for them to read. After checking understanding and highlighting key language items, tell them to transform the piece into a different text type, e.g. if it reports a chemical spill, divide the class into 'residents' and 'owners of the polluting factory'. Get the 'residents' to write a complaint to the 'owners', who answer the message, etc. Or ask them to write an interview between a reporter and a resident, a report by a police officer, etc.
- Ask learners to change the location of a story and then think about what other changes would be needed in consequence.
- Ask learners to move the story to a different time period. What would happen if a story from today's world had taken place in the Middle Ages? What would be different? This kind of transformation is best done when learners are learning about a historical period in another subject.
- Ask learners to write a prequel or sequel; that is, what happens before or after the story they have read.
- Ask learners to change the gender of one of the protagonists and rewrite the story from that person's viewpoint.

Text transformations are also an ideal link between the skills of writing and of reading. I have found the reference below a very useful read.

Brassell, D. and Rasinski,T. (2008) *Comprehension That Works: Taking Students Beyond Ordinary Understanding to Deep Comprehension.* Shell Educational Publishing.

Engage learners in silent dialogue writing

> Interactive writing can help learners pay attention to what another person communicates to them and come up with spontaneous and creative ideas.

In developing learners' speaking skills, one of the biggest challenges can be to get them to communicate with each other as themselves, rather than acting out dialogues they have studied beforehand. Writing can make important contributions towards spontaneous communication. Here's a powerful and engaging idea.

- Think up a situation two people could be involved in, a situation that has the potential to deeply engage your learners. On one sheet of paper for each pair of learners, write an opening line for a dialogue that could take place in that situation, e.g. Mum: *What a fine time to finally get home!*

- With learners in pairs, give each one a role and a brief description of the situation, e.g. *One of you is a teenager, the other one their mum. It's 10:30 pm, and the teen's just come home, tiptoeing into the house ...*

- Hand out the paper with the dialogue opener, giving it to the 'teen' in each pair. Ask them to quickly write an answer without the 'mum' seeing what the 'teen' is writing. The teen then hands over the paper to the mum, who writes her next response, then hands the sheet of paper back to the teen and so on. Tell learners to keep communicating in this way with each other until the dialogue comes to a natural halt.

- Then ask learners to go through the dialogue together and check for clarity, and decide how they could improve it, helping each other.

- Next, get learners to turn the paper over and re-create the conversation with each other, using what they remember as a guide. Tell them it doesn't matter if they deviate from the model, as they could not possibly keep to it word for word anyway.

- Then learners swap roles and write another dialogue. This time the new 'mum' should start, writing their own dialogue opener.

77 Use grammar poetry to make language more memorable

> Many teens like poetry. Few like grammar. Letting learners play with language can help them remember grammar.

Short poems with a repetitive structure can help learners remember lexico-grammatical chunks and, if used appropriately, can transfer to the learners' own writing. A type of activity well suited to help with that transfer is the *dictogloss*. It's not new, but in workshops I have often been surprised to find how few colleagues use it with their learners.

This is how I introduce it to my teenage learners: *I'm going to give you a dictogloss. What does the word remind you of? ... Yes, that's right, dictation. And it* is *a kind of dictation, but you're not allowed to write anything down while I'm dictating. Then jot down as much as you can remember. Finally, with a partner reconstruct the original text.*

See Appendix 2 for a short grammar dictogloss for a class whose learners have problems with the use of possessive *-s* versus ... *of* ... .

After four or five minutes ask the class to dictate the text back to you while you write it on the board.

Then do a gradual deletion activity. Read the text out to the class. Then delete a word or a chunk. Ask a learner to 'read out' the text from memory as if you hadn't deleted anything. Continue until the text has disappeared and they can recall it from memory.

Next, give learners a few prompts – *What's ...? My ...* etc. – and ask them to write their own poem, keeping to the basic structure of the model text.

You can find a whole range of lesson plans complete with model poems in the reference below.

Gerngross, G., Puchta, H. and Thornbury, S. (2006) *Teaching Grammar Creatively.* Helbling Languages.

Mini-sagas

> **Teenagers can be reluctant when it comes to writing.**
> **Writing a mini-saga will almost certainly energise them.**

Mini-sagas became popular in the UK when the *Sunday Telegraph* launched a competition to write short stories of exactly 50 words. The title can contain up to five more words. A mini-saga must tell a real story, complete with a beginning, a middle and an end, often with a twist.

When I discovered their secret

'Aliens?' the headmaster smiled. I needed to talk to the police. 'Watched too much science fiction?' the detective laughed. I felt like an idiot. Then, walking past his office window five minutes later, I overheard his phone conversation with the headmaster. 'We need to leave. They know who we are!'

To introduce mini-saga writing in your class:

- Hand out a copy of a mini-saga to your learners. Use the one above if you like. Tell them that this is a text that had been created for a writing competition in a UK newspaper. Don't tell them the rules – yet. Ask them to read the text, then discuss with a partner what they think the rules were that writers had to keep to. Ask for their suggestions. If necessary, explain the rules.
- Give a theme (*Vampires* is popular with teens, and so are *Friendship*, *Love*, *A Dream* and *Courage*); or ask learners to choose their own.
- Tell learners they should write a short story first, without counting the words, and then trim it down (works well on a computer).
- Explain that shorter sentences often work better. They should note that *I have got* is three words but *I've got* is two, and make a surprise ending.

For more on using mini-sagas with your learners, see the blog below.

....

Cox, M. *Teaching Your Pupils How to Write a Mini Saga*. Available at: https://www.cambridge.org/us/education/blog/mini-sagas

> Most teens have heroes – sports professionals, pop stars, actors, influencers, etc. Teens identify with their heroes. They use them as 'projection screens' – projecting key human qualities onto their idols.

Teens, although they often appear so cool, can suffer from lots of insecurities. For them, identifying with celebrities is a way of getting in touch with qualities they believe these stars have – for example, courage, genius, love, creativity, friendship, endurance. So, from a teen perspective, the celebrities help them succeed in a threatening world.

- Ask learners to call out the name of their favourite celebrity. Keep a tally on the board to find the most popular one.
- Now ask the learners to work in pairs. Hand out slips of paper, about five per pair. Tell them to imagine their celebrity is coming for an interview. Ask them to write questions.
- Depending on the level of the class, write a few prompts on the board. A teacher in an A2 class wrote this:

  What's your favourite ...?   *What do you think about ...?*
  Do you really ...?   *What's the secret of your success?*
  Is it true that you ...?   *Do you get lots of messages on ...?*
  How do you like ...?   *Can I ask you a personal question?*
  Are you ...?

- Walk round, help learners if necessary and tell them not to write their names on the slips.
- Ask learners to drop their slips in a shoebox. Ask one of them to bring a photo of the winning celebrity to the class for the next lesson.
- At the start of that lesson, ask a learner to come to the front of the class and be the celebrity.
- Ask learners to draw slips from the box and ask the question. The celebrity has to answer every question – and invent an answer if they don't know it.

An alternative that usually creates a lot of fun is the class writing questions for the *least* popular celebrity.

List-writing is popular among teens, especially if you give them a task that is a bit wacky. You may be surprised how creative some of them will be.

Teens like writing lists: *my ten favourite movies*; *eight things to eat while studying*, etc. You should be able to find lots more examples on the internet.

- Tell your learners that they are going to write a list of, say, six things they would take on a trip to Mars. Tell them they should think up five to ten items and make each item a headline. Then they should write a short paragraph that explains the headline:

Six things I'd take with me on a trip to Mars

1 **My comb**
I love combs. I've always loved them. And recently I found MY comb in a hairdresser's in London. It's blue. *I had* to buy it – blue's my favourite colour. I couldn't do without it!

2 **Cashew nuts**
My utterly fave snack. Imagine looking out of the window of the spacecraft and watching the Earth getting smaller and smaller, while wolfing a bagful of cashew nuts!

- Write three themes on the board; your learners choose one. (Remember that having a choice usually motivates teens a lot.) Here are some themes your learners could write lists about. Depending on their age and cultural background, you might want to make changes or come up with your own ideas:
  - Things I would never wear to school
  - Ice-cream flavours nobody has ever eaten
  - Things I could train a parrot to do
  - Reasons why the chicken crossed the road
  - Places where I would *never* want to spend a holiday
  - Reasons why I would refuse a million dollars
  - Things to do with an empty notebook

81 Use mentor sentences to inspire your learners' writing

> Mentor sentences come from the writings of published authors and are used to enrich the learners' own writing.

Here are a few ideas for you to try out with your learners:

- Search literary texts for a model sentence to help your learners enrich their own writing. I recommend young adult novels. Many of them are accessible for B1, some even for A2 learners.
- Write the sentence on the board. Draw attention to the impact it is likely to create in the reader's mind, and how it achieves that. The example is from Mari Mancusi's *Boys that bite*, and was chosen to help learners get more variety into their opening sentences:
  You know, being bitten by a vampire one week before prom really sucks.
  Then delete one word at a time and each time ask learners to say the whole sentence until they can recall it from memory.
- Ask learners to write a new sentence following the structure of the mentor sentence. Give them a topic or let them choose. Here are two produced by B1 learners, based on the example above:
  You know, being attacked by a dog on the first day of your holiday really frightens you.
  Well, being told by your parents of their divorce one week before Christmas totally hurts.
- Ask learners to go through stories they've written over time, pick one and create a sentence based on the structure of the mentor sentence that could be inserted to enrich the text they wrote.
- For a few weeks, set aside ten minutes every other lesson to work with mentor sentences.
- Alternatively, you can use the mentor sentence idea to help learners take ownership of specific grammar constructions, e.g. *If only I'd* ... . Sites such as ludwig.guru will retrieve authentic sentences that include the search structure and often give alternatives too.

Ask learners to write an eyewitness account

> It's important for learners to learn to write in different
> text genres. Report writing is often regarded as not very
> motivating, so the ideas here show that it can be.

It is often difficult for learners to differentiate between observations and interpretations.

Rather than telling them about the differences, you could invite a friend (who is not known to your learners) to come to your class at an agreed point in time, do something unexpected, and swiftly leave again. At that moment you should have left the classroom for a very short while, telling learners you need to see the head, or similar excuse (or at the very least have your back turned at the far end of the room).

Let's imagine your friend goes to the board and writes: *NOBODY KNOWS I WAS HERE.* Or puts on your desk a gift-wrapped box with a ribbon around it. Or (if you think this is not too much!) they could take your jacket, which you have hung over your chair, before leaving.

Your learners will be eager to tell you what happened. Tell them that you're confused and want them to write a precise report of the incident. You might like to offer a few prompts, e.g. *What happened? When did it happen? Where did it happen? Who was involved? What did the person look like? What was he/she wearing?*

After learners have written their eyewitness accounts, ask them to read them out. On the board, make notes that show the differences between the learners' observations (what they saw) and their interpretations (their own thinking about their observations).

Ask learners to think about their interpretations of the incident. Ask them why they think the person acted the way they did, etc.

After this initial surprise visit you could use short video clips to further develop the learners' ability to focus their observations and write them down as well as learning to differentiate between observations and interpretations. Teach them to use concrete observations as a basis for their interpretations, rather than just imagination or intuition.

H: Behaviour management

The non-verbal communications expert Michael Grinder
once said, 'If you can teach teenagers, you can teach
anyone!' That's true of what we see in many teenage
classrooms, and every teacher of teens knows how
challenging they can be at times. Provocative and disruptive
behaviour, aggressive language, inability or unwillingness
to pay attention, lack of persistence when it comes to
homework, problems with phones during class – the list
goes on. In this section, we look at all these and other
issues, and suggest practical things we can do to help
and deal with the difficulties, being understanding and
supportive, yet firm and fair.

> Learners sitting still with their backs straight may give
> the impression they're paying attention, but there is no
> guarantee that this is actually the case.

In an experiment a few years ago (see reference below), a dull two-and-a-half-minute voice message was played to a group of 40 people. Half the group was invited to do a kind of doodling activity while listening, and the other half was told to sit still. Neither group knew there would be a memory test afterwards. When asked about details from the recording, the doodlers remembered 29% more details than those in the other group.

This shows that our beliefs about what paying attention involves may not always be right. It appears that when we're bored and about to switch off, doodling can in fact keep us alert and attentive.

Share this information with your learners and ask them whether they believe doodling while listening may influence their own retention. Then get them to try it, and see whether what they'd thought was right.

Drinking water, eating a snack and chewing gum could have an equally positive effect, by the way. I am aware, however, that might be a bit too far – although your learners might find that cool!

When my sons were teens and wanted to listen to music while doing homework, I was strictly against it. It has been shown, however, that the type of task, one's personality and the type of music may influence the outcomes in different ways. So why not ask your learners to experiment with listening to music while doing their homework?

Pillay, S. (2016) 'The "thinking" benefits of doodling.' Harvard Health Blog. Available at: https://www.health.harvard.edu/blog/the-thinking-benefits-of-doodling-2016121510844

84 Problems with homework? Don't give up!

> I believe homework is important, and it's worth doing our best to help learners be prepared to dedicate some of their time to it.

If you want your learners to do their homework, there are various preconditions you have to keep in mind:

- Homework needs to be relevant to learners. This will be more likely the case when it is a continuation of something you have been working on in class.
- Alternatively, ask learners to do some work that will be needed in a future lesson, e.g. some research on a topic you are going to deal with. Or when you have asked them to, for example, write a text, then make sure their efforts are read by other learners and you, and that the writers get feedback. Ideally, learners should feel they have accomplished something by doing their homework, or that they have made a contribution to the (next) lesson.
- Homework needs to be doable; in other words, you need to make sure learners understand what they are supposed to be doing. Tell learners early on what their homework is; at the end of the lesson their level of attention may be lower.
- Every now and then, give learners the choice of at least two options for their homework (see **33** on the importance of giving learners choices).
- Most teens love cooperating and being in touch with their classmates on the phone or the internet. So, pair your learners up occasionally, to work on their homework together.
- Make sure learners have made a note of the homework. Discuss with them how long they reckon the homework will take them and then ask them afterwards whether their estimate was realistic. Make sure that the homework you give them is reasonable, timewise.
- Discuss with learners whether a texted homework reminder would be useful. If the consensus is yes, then agree on a buddy system for sending the texts.

Use specific language strategies to stop disruptive behaviour

> When learners are behaving disruptively, the language you use can have a powerful effect on how they feel and react to your intervention.

Studies have shown that teachers who are better at handling difficult situations in teenage classrooms use specific language patterns that seem to result in their learners feeling more respected and reacting less confrontationally. The three strategies presented here (see the reference below) are examples of such teacher interventions.

1 In order to depersonalise a situation and treat a learner respectfully at the same time, use a language pattern that describes what happens when they show an (unwanted) behaviour and what behaviour you want to see instead. Use: *When you do X, this happens*. Rather than saying: *Stop playing with your ruler*, say: *Peter, when you play with your ruler, others are disturbed and can't focus on their writing task. Please work more quietly*. Then towards the end of the intervention nod your head – that gives the impression that you trust the learner to behave properly.

2 Don't ask questions when you actually want to give instructions. Avoid saying things like: *Can't you hear what I'm saying? Do you really want to disturb us all the time? How often do I have to tell you that you should stop speaking* [your own language] *in the English class?* As Plevin (2019) says, 'Simple, concise directions delivered calmly and deliberately will work much more effectively than questions if you want students to meet your expectations with minimum fuss.' So instead say: *Stop talking now. Focus on your task and start writing*.

3 Use *thank you* instead of *please* in connection with a direct instruction. *Stop talking.* <slight pause> *Thank you*, can be more powerful than: *Stop talking, please*.

Plevin, R. (2019) *Take Control of the Noisy Class* (pp. 59–60). Life Raft Media. Kindle Edition.

86 Don't let conflicts escalate – make your learners think

> Teenage behaviour can become provocative or disruptive. When that happens, it's better to treat learners with respect rather than putting them down.

Behind provocation, disruption, truancy, cheating, lying, aggression – even abuse of alcohol/drugs – there often lurks a lack of self-esteem. The trouble is, those behaviours risk generating punishment and interventions that negatively impact the learner's self-esteem. A vicious circle.

So, avoid standoffs in class. You may, perfectly understandably, feel you should express your anger, but a public showdown rarely leads to constructive development. Breathe slowly and keep calm. Quietly tell the learner you'll see them after class. At that point, don't tell them off, but say, e.g. *I wonder when we could have a chat to see what we can do to improve the situation?* Arrange a meeting in a private, quiet corner.

The meeting is best conducted in the learner's language. If you don't speak the learner's language, things are more challenging. One option is to ask a colleague to mediate the conversation. They must obviously speak the learner's L1, and should be accepted by the learner, too.

Avoid *You*-messages, e.g. *You really misbehaved last lesson. You'll have to stop that kind of behaviour, otherwise I'll … .* Instead, use *I*-messages to give feedback and express how you felt, e.g. *What I saw reminded me of when I was a teen and I used that kind of language – but afterwards I never felt good about it. A situation like the one we had is difficult for me. I'd wanted to know what you guys thought of the story we read, but things didn't work the way I had envisaged. Then I felt hurt, and confused. I wonder how you see things now …?* Chances are the learner will feel grateful for not being told off or punished, and will react with some insight. If so, ask them how they could have behaved in class instead.

Then get the learner to agree on some concrete steps of behaviour – and follow up with another chat to monitor the situation, give feedback and praise!

Learners are shouting out the answer? Vary the expected response

> Neurobiologists say that knowing an answer makes teens so excited that they need to shout it out – so they can relax again.

It's good to establish a calm class, but insisting on learners raising their hands and waiting patiently for you to allow them to speak could kill their enthusiasm. So try a range of different strategies to elicit a variety of responses.

- Tell learners that you are going to ask them a question and they should think of their answer. If it is yes, they stand up; if no, they stay seated. Then you will invite them in turn to explain their answers and give concrete examples for their reasoning.
- Tell learners to turn to a partner and find a joint answer. Say that once they have finished, you will ask five pairs for their answer.
- Present a whole set of questions to learners at a time. Ask them to work out the answers, and say you'll listen to their suggestions.
- At the beginning of the lesson, write a brainteaser on the board, e.g. *What is the odd one out in this list: calf – kid – pony – cub?* (Pony, a small horse; the rest are young animals.) Tell learners that you will ask for their answers two minutes before the lesson ends. Tell them that they may chat to a partner about the riddle, as long as they do that very quietly and as long as they speak in English.
- Tell learners that this time they can all shout out their answers at the same time, but when you hold your index finger in front of your lips, they need to be silent. Ask your question. Allow a maximum of 20 seconds of chaos. It can be fun to ask afterwards what they think other kids have shouted out.

Gilbert, I., Curran, A. and Supple, M. (2006) *Three Chairs, a Table and a Lamp: Or how insights from neuroscience can improve the quality of learning in our schools.* Crown House Publishing.

88 Avoid conflicts around mobile phones

> Clear rules for the use of phones in class can help avoid conflict.

There is evidence that teens' often excessive time spent on social media can thwart our attempts to help them grow into mature adults, as 'it is the dumb, novelty-seeking portion of the brain driving the limbic system that induces this feeling of pleasure, not the … higher-level thought centers in the prefrontal cortex. … E-mail, Facebook, and Twitter checking constitute a neural addiction' (Levitin, D. 1994).

On the other hand, phones can support the learners' learning in a positive way:

- Introduce a general rule about phone use, e.g. learners are to put their (clearly identifiable) phones in a basket (or switch them to silent) unless you specifically allow their use (by showing a sign of a person making a phone call).
- Learners can use the timer on their phones to keep to time limits when, e.g. doing a writing task. This helps them be more focused.
- Encourage learners to take photos as a memory aid, e.g. a poster they have created during group work, words you have written on the board during a brainstorming phase, etc. They can draw on these photographic notes for their homework.
- Give two or three learners a research task on something they have come across and ask them to report their findings to the class.
- From time to time, give learners two or three minutes to text each other – in English. Tell them beforehand you will be carrying out random checks that they are keeping to this rule, and a violation of it will lead to a ban of mobile use for a number of lessons.
- Suggest learners record you when you're, e.g. reading out a paragraph from a text, so they can use this for their homework.
- Get learners to produce short videos of interviews with classmates, mini-talks, etc.

Levitin, D. (2015) *The Organized Mind: Thinking Straight in the Age of Information Overload*. Penguin Books Ltd. Kindle Edition.

Help learners solve conflicts in constructive ways

> Conflicts are part of being human, but very few teens have learnt how to resolve them in a positive way.

The way you deal with learners' conflicts is a powerful model for their own behaviour. When you are faced with learners quarrelling, you need to be, and be seen to be, objective. Avoid asking *Why*-questions, e.g. *Why are you shouting at Sandra?* If you do, you risk being drawn into the dynamics of mutual blame – *Yes, you did. No, I didn't* – with everyone defending themselves.

Instead, ask each learner in turn what happened, and facilitate an exchange of viewpoints by calmly asking questions along the lines of: *So how did you feel about that? And how did you think that made Annabel feel? How could you have acted differently in that situation and still expressed your feelings?*

Make sure learners understand that it's normal to have conflicts, and that we can learn how to resolve them. Tell them that they are entitled to have feelings, and that it's important to describe them – calmly – in words. Angry accusations and sulking are not good ways to solve a conflict. Hence, share with your learners that reality is different from our individual perceptions of reality and that, in order to resolve a conflict, it's important to understand the other person's viewpoint. Teach learners how to negotiate and how to find compromises. It's important for them to understand that we can't always win and sometimes, in order to resolve a conflict, the most helpful thing is to give the other person what they want.

Then help learners understand that once a conflict has been resolved, it is counterproductive to hang onto negative feelings only to bring them up again later! Also, teach learners the difference between conflicts and violence. Say that we have choices in how we deal with conflicts. Tell them that you will never tolerate any violence at all and if somebody becomes violent, tell them clearly what the consequences will be, according to the school policy.

90 Have strategies ready to deal with attention-seekers

> Some of our learners' most bothersome behaviour is seeking our attention overmuch. It's useful to have strategies ready to deal with that.

There are learners who will do anything to attract your attention. That often gets them negative attention – which may be the opposite of what they would like to achieve. Here are a few suggestions on how to deal with attention-seekers.

- Nominate individuals when asking questions, preferably **after** the question: *What's the past of 'catch'? – Oskar?* This will limit the degree to which the attention-seeker can participate.
- Acknowledge an attention-seeker's contribution but move on quickly: *Thank you, Roberto. Anyone else have an opinion?*
- Experience has shown that it can be better to use tactical ignoring, together with some proximity praise – i.e. acting as if you hadn't noticed the behaviour while praising other learners for doing their work. *Thank you, guys, for putting a lot of effort into getting this right. Nick, it's great you've finished reading already*, etc. However, the attention-seeker may continue with his behaviour (yes, it's usually a boy). In that case, like it or not, you'll need to activate the consequences that you'll have clearly warned him of beforehand, so he knows what to expect, e.g. see you after class / see the headmaster / do a special assignment in another class / you inform his parents.
- Plevin (2018) advises keeping calm when you activate the consequences: '… just take the wind out of his sails with the following lines: *I've told you what is happening, you made your choice. If you want to talk more about this we can do it later; come and see me after school, I'll be in my room. Now get on with your work.* … and then turn your back, … and march off into the sunset. Or back to your desk, whichever is nearer.'

Plevin, R. (2018) *The Behaviour Tool Kit: The ultimate collection of answers to your most frustrating classroom management problems and questions.* Kindle Edition.

> **When a learner gets angry, the last thing we need to do is show anger ourselves.**

Anger comes from engaging the amygdala – an almond-shaped structure in the human brain, primarily involved in the processing of emotional responses such as aggression, fear, guilt, shame and anxiety – and usually leads to fight, flight or freeze behaviour. In learners, this causes them to become aggressive, miss classes, stop working or withdraw from the lesson. Knowing that the teen brain is at a stage that makes them tend to behave irrationally can help us understand what's going on.

But amygdala-controlled behaviour is not something we ourselves want to display, especially in confrontational situations. After all, we have a well-developed prefrontal cortex that allows us to make rational decisions rather than react emotionally.

There is often little we can do to calm down a learner directly when they are upset or angry. Sometimes, it's best to breathe calmly and acknowledge their emotions. Suggesting the learner might relax a bit is a good strategy, too. Or saying, e.g. *I can see how angry this has made you. Take a minute or two to sit down and wait for things to calm down a bit.*

It can be useful to change the subject: *Yes, I can see this isn't working well. So let's go for something completely different.* This could be an effective way of defusing the situation.

While things are going well in general, it's a good idea to win over difficult learners by giving them special responsibilities, e.g. setting up technical equipment. And make a point of finding out what they're good at, and interested in, so that you can chat with them about things they like.

If you are looking for more suggestions on how to deal with difficult classes, I'd like to recommend Plevin (2018) – see the reference on the previous page.

When learners are verbally aggressive – go meta

> Teens can be confrontational and rude to each other.
> We need to know how to deal with these situations.

One way of dealing with verbal aggression is going meta – inviting learners to look at a problem from 'outside', considering the effects of the action. That often takes the heat out of difficult situations. Aggressive verbal behaviour in teenage groups tends to be a male way of establishing the individual's position in the herd. Research shows that it is people with high testosterone (i.e. teen boys) who are likely to react aggressively to threatening and stressful situations such as one-on-one confrontations. This doesn't mean, however, that girls never use such behaviour. Here are a few suggestions for what you could do:

- Stay calm – even if what was said was very inappropriate. In such situations, teens tend to use words that they use among themselves. So while you may be shocked, the class might not. Say something along the lines of: *OK, guys, I see this is a difficult situation. Let's just breathe slowly and count up to ten. Let's take a bit of time.* <pause> *I'm sure we can work this out.*
- Draw two stick figures on the board, each with a letter standing for a student in the confrontation. Say: *This is James. And here's Tom. What's going on here? Let's think for a moment. How does Tom feel? And what does he have in mind? And James? I'd like to ask you all first, before we ask James and Tom for their points of view.*
- Carry on: *Let's think about this a bit. Conflict is normal when humans are together. So, what could James and Tom do to make the situation better? And how can we help?*
- Write the suggestions on the board in a non-judgemental way. Then ask: *What could he do? Would any of the suggestions on the board work for him? Or for him?*

Gilbert, I., Curran, A. and Supple, M. (2006) *Three Chairs, A Table and a Lamp: Or how insights from neuroscience can improve the quality of learning in our schools.* Crown House Publishing.

I: Fostering maturity

Despite the fact that teens tend to mature physically at a younger age than they used to, their mental maturity lags way behind. Research shows that the development of the so-called frontal lobe of the neocortex – that is, the structure in the brain required for higher-order thinking, decision making, critical thinking and the willingness to take responsibility for oneself and others – tends to be delayed into their twenties or later. Further, many teens depend heavily on digital social media that can so often create a deceptive sense of accomplishment in them. The tips in this section include ones that will help teens to set realistic goals for themselves and learn to be persistent, defeat procrastination, develop a growth mindset and use efficient study strategies; in short, to work towards becoming responsible adults.

93 Help learners to set goals and reach them

> When we ask learners to set goals, they will often do so quite enthusiastically. However, most learners tend to forget about them when they come up against obstacles.

In order to help learners retain their vision of those goals, try these ideas:

- Write or project a text with keywords learners might need in order to talk about their goals, in, e.g. vocabulary, pronunciation, reading, listening, speaking, writing, preparing for exams, studying for tests, getting good grades, etc.
- Give learners an example of a goal and concrete action steps. For example, Goal: *I will increase my knowledge of vocabulary*. Action steps: *Every day we have English, I'll take five minutes to go over new language I have learnt that day, and another 10 to revise language previously learnt. I'll do that for two weeks, starting dd/mm*. Ask learners to work in groups and define more goals and action steps. Help them phrase these well, and write them on the board. Ask all learners to note them down.
- Tell learners to write down examples of what a learner might get out of achieving a goal, e.g. *My parents will allow me to spend more time with my friends*.
- Ask learners to think up reasons they might not stick to their goal, e.g. *I might forget about* [my goal], and a strategy to overcome that obstacle, e.g. *I'll put a note in my calendar to remind me of* [my goal].
- Offer individual feedback to your learners who write up, at home, (1) a goal, (2) the best outcome they could get from achieving it, and (3) concrete action steps to reach that goal, together with (4) what might stop them and (5) a strategy they could use to overcome that obstacle.
- Encourage those learners who have a clear strategy to use it and talk to you regularly about how well it works.

Steinberg, L. (2014) *Age of Opportunity. Lessons from the New Science of Adolescence*. Boston and New York: Mariner Books.

Help learners become responsible adults

There is evidence that these days it takes teens until their mid-twenties or later to become mature. Prediction and hypothesising tasks help develop their cognition.

Studies show that teens' limbic (emotional) system develops faster than their prefrontal cortex (needed for logical-critical thinking). This can predispose them to be emotion-driven and risk-taking, and to act without thinking.

AI researcher Jeff Hawkins (2004) says that at the root of human intelligence is a memory-prediction system. Which is what's needed here. To help it develop, we could give learners prediction tasks:

- List the classroom chores. Engage learners in *What if?* thinking: *Somebody has to water the flowers regularly. What if they forget? The flowers will die. OK, what if they die?* etc. Write language prompts on the board if necessary.
- Remind learners of a current social or global issue. Predict how you think it may develop. Then ask for their predictions.
- Ask learners to take turns preparing interesting or humorous present, future and past *What if ...?* questions for the class, e.g. *What if I phoned the police and told them I'd been threatened by a cactus?*
- Tell a story. When you've finished, tell learners to ask you *What would have happened if ...?* questions. If necessary, give prompts.
- In a consecutive lesson, tell another story. It's your turn to ask learners questions. Finally, get them to tell each other stories in groups or pairs and ask questions.

Hawkins, J. (2004) *On Intelligence.* New York: St. Martin's Griffin.

95 Help learners beat procrastination

> Procrastination often results in learners failing to do their homework, revise for tests, etc. So it's well worth equipping your learners with ways they can deal with it themselves.

Procrastination seems to afflict teens in particular. There are many reasons why teens procrastinate: their newfound freedom to spend a lot of time on social media, to hang out with friends, and the inclination to postpone tasks they see as demanding or boring. Eventually, however, pressure tends to build up and they begin to feel very stressed.

The following routine is based on a suggestion by Jane Nelsen (2012).

- Suggest to your learners that they each write a list of four *would-love-to-do* after-school activities, and a list of their *have-to-do-but-not-keen* ones. Imagine a learner has *hang out with friends, play my favourite digital game, play football* and *watch YouTube videos* on one list, and *study for the maths test* on the other. Ask them to plan their afternoon in such a way that they include all the activities (including the *must-do*) on their lists. You'll often find that they keep the must-do activities for last.

- Tell learners that experience has shown that people who successfully do their must-do activities often go through a process of negotiating a deal with themselves. Show them that they could make an agreement with themselves, for example, to do the must-do first, so they can really enjoy the others; or to do two activities they like first, then do the must-do one, and then the other two they like, keeping their favourite activity for last.

- Later, ask your learners how things are working out for them. If more help is needed, you may want to give them another idea, such as doing the must-do activities with a friend. Teens like working together, and they don't usually want to let a friend down. Once they have agreed to meet up for study, they will probably want to keep their word!

Nelsen, J. (2012) *Positive Discipline for Teenagers. Revised 3rd Edition.* Harmony Books. Kindle Edition.

Inspire learners to become high achievers

Teens tend to admire (or envy) classmates who consistently learn fast and achieve top results. You can show learners how to push themselves beyond their self-created false limits and become high achievers too.

Teenagers are fascinated by extremes. Bathla (2020) uses the amazing story of Göran Kropp to illustrate how anybody can achieve top performance if they become aware of their self-created false limits, then create goals, and make efforts to achieve them. Göran rode his bike from Sweden to the Himalayas, summited Everest solo without oxygen, descended, and cycled some of the way back home.

If your learners want to push beyond their limits too, reading, listening to and telling inspiring stories like the one about Göran Kropp can instil the same values. Another way would be to use the strategies below:

- Visualise again and again doing the action(s) you need to take to achieve your goal. Tell yourself repeatedly, 'I do this all the time. This is who I am!'
- When doubts creep in, make sure you immediately replace them with thoughts about how to achieve your goal.
- Distractions come not only from your own mind but also from outside, e.g. you're set to study this evening when a friend invites you to the movies. Don't react impulsively. Become aware that there is always a moment between a distraction and your reaction. Use that time gap to make a decision you won't regret later. Think of your goal and ask yourself, 'What's Important Now?' This is the WIN strategy.
- Keep your goal in mind, focus on your task and replace any distracting thought as soon as it comes up. Practise regularly. Switch off your phone while you are practising. Notice how you enjoy it more and more.

I learnt the suggestions above from Som Bathla (see the reference below).

Bathla, S. (2020) *Trigger High Performance: Upgrade Your Mind, Learn Effectively to Become an Expert, Activate Flow State to Take Relentless Action, and Perform at Your Best* (Personal Mastery Series Book 3). Kindle Edition.

97 Deriving pride from effort – and learning from mistakes

> Teachers tend to praise or reprimand learners according to their results. But we can help our learners better if we focus on their learning process.

As a young teacher it took me a while to understand that the more I developed an interest in helping the not-so-successful learners too, the more gratifying I found it.

- Praise your learners' *efforts*, their *improvements* and their *perseverance*.
- Teach learners to see their mistakes in a different way: do lots of practice tests with them (see **100** on study strategies). Ask them to go over their errors after each test and reflect on what they've learnt from making those mistakes. Useful language: *Today I learned that I need to … . In future I'm going to try to … .*
- Discuss with your class what connection they see between their efforts to learn and their future. *If I know how to … I'll be able to … . I think it's useful to … because … .*
- Share stories of your own teenage years, telling them about things you learnt then that are important for you now.
- Make sure you never criticise any learners in front of others, or when you're in a bad mood. And always ensure your criticism is descriptive, not judgemental. Say, for example, *I've noticed you've got problems applying what we discussed about the present perfect. How can I help you with this?* Don't say, for example, *You've made lots of mistakes with the present perfect. This is **not** a good result.* If you consistently give learners feedback in a non-judgemental way, they will begin to see you as a person who helps them improve their performance and believes in their ability to learn and grow.
- Don't praise learners for *not* making mistakes. If any learners have got everything right, claiming that they didn't have to study at all, apologise, tongue in cheek, for having given them too easy a task. Promise that next time you'll give them a more challenging task, so they can learn from it.

Coach body language clusters

Teens often acquire an interest in psychology. So body language is often a popular – and useful – topic.

Ask your learners to work in pairs/small groups to brainstorm the facial expressions of a happy person and a depressed one. Help them with language, e.g. *They look … . They have … . Their X is/are* [adjective]. *They* [verb] [adverb] … . Then encourage them to extend this to the whole body.

As an optional activity, you could divide your class in two groups. Group A models a body language cluster typical of people who are happy: head up, regular eye contact with others, smiles, shoulders straight, a light step. Group B models a negative mood: head down, no eye contact, frowns, shoulders down, a shuffling step. Ask learners to stand up and walk around within their group like that for three minutes. They then swap roles. Finally, ask what they have noticed about their emotions. Chances are quite a few of them will report that their emotions were influenced by their body language.

Ask learners to observe different clusters of body language while sitting in class. Sitting with their upper body slightly forward gives the impression they are interested, but at the same time influences their brain so they *become* more interested. Tell them to keep eye contact with the speaker, and occasionally nod their head to signal they are following.

At the KIPP Academy (a charter school chain in the USA) teachers use the acronym SLANT to remind learners of key behaviour in class: S = Sit up; L = Listen; A = Ask questions; N = Nod; T = Track the speaker with your eyes. The 'nod' instruction is interesting since a nod while listening can subtly direct the speaker's attention, creating a positive pairing.

Help learners develop growth mindsets

> Learners with fixed mindsets believe they have a certain amount of intelligence, talent, etc., and that can't be changed. We can help them change their attitude into a healthier one.

We want learners to develop a growth mindset – the belief that they can cultivate their qualities and capabilities through their efforts. These tips will help do that, and have been influenced by suggestions from Carol Dweck's website (see reference below).

Cut out speech bubbles from poster paper. Write the following statements on the board and ask learners to react to them:

- *It's all the teacher's fault. The test was much too difficult.*
- *I'm a loser when it comes to language learning. A complete loser!*
- *I got a lot wrong this time. But I'll learn from my mistakes.*
- *We haven't got a lot of time to prepare, but I'll try.*

Learners are probably going to say that some are negative and some positive. Ask them to arrange them in two columns: *fixed mindset* and *growth mindset*. Say that people's mindsets often determine their inner monologues and that people with a growth mindset believe they can become better through their own efforts. (This may need to be discussed in the learners' L1.)

Tell learners that one way of dealing with fixed mindsets is 'talking back', e.g.

> Fixed mindset: *You might fail – then the others will laugh at you.*
> Growth mindset: *So what? Most successful people failed many times in their lives. They succeeded because they didn't give up.*
> Fixed mindset: *This is **the teacher's** fault. The test was unfair.*
> Growth mindset: *A way I can improve is by taking the responsibility for my own failure. I'll make a plan with definite action points so I can do better next time.*

Dweck, C. *Mindset: The Nature of Change*. Available at:
http://mindsetonline.com/changeyourmindset/natureofchange/index.html

Teach efficient study strategies

> **Many learners don't know how to prepare efficiently for exams. We can help them.**

Young people need to develop three sets of cognitive skills: cognitive flexibility (very important for, e.g. preparing for a test and doing it), working memory (to hold key information in mind in order to complete the test) and inhibitory control (helps to avoid being distracted while doing the test).

Study strategies lie within cognitive flexibility. There is solid research evidence (see Dunlosky et al. 2013) to show which strategies are most efficient. It also shows that learners who achieve good test results in lower grades can have problems later on, when in control of their own learning. So if you teach good study strategies – a quick and easy task – this can be very helpful in the long term as well. The basic strategies are:

1   Make it a habit to review new learning from *every* lesson.
2   When preparing for a test, *space* your learning, i.e. study regularly, in small chunks, over a longer period of time, not just the evening before the test.
3   Forget highlighting, underlining, re-reading, etc. Instead, do *practice tests*. Test yourself, or work with a partner and test each other (see **21**). Repeat the same tests several times to see yourself improving! And remember: the more 'minds-on' learning you do, the better. Challenge yourself. You can do it!

Dunlosky, J., Rawson, K. A., Marsh, E. J., Nathan, M. J. and Willingham, D. T. (2013) 'Improving students' learning with effective learning techniques: promising directions from cognitive and educational psychology.' *Psychological Science in the Public Interest.* 14(1), 4–48.

Puchta, H. (2020) *Cognitive control functions in language learning.* Cambridge: Cambridge University Press. Available at: https://www.cambridge.org/us/files/9515/9242/5077/Cambridge_Papers_ELT_Cog_Control_Functions_minipaper.pdf

101   Help your learners be happy learners

> People can see their work as a job, a career or a calling.
> Learners' attitudes to their studies can vary similarly.

Some learners just want to get through school, expecting nothing much from it. Others see the progress they make and the skills they develop as important for their careers. Yet others are passionate about school and totally committed to learning, actively exploring the intellectual and social opportunities they are given. To help learners develop the third attitude, try these ideas, based on the chapter 'Habits for Professional Happiness' in Bathla, S. (2019).

- Dictate the seven habits that help create happiness. Make it a habit to:
    1   be a few minutes early for school and any meetings;
    2   start any communication positively;
    3   get into a flow every day;
    4   make sure you recover from stress;
    5   accept and learn from your teachers' advice and feedback;
    6   build a network of resourceful people;
    7   look for opportunities to help others.

- In pairs, learners discuss how these habits contribute to happiness.
- Ask learners to report their findings. Take notes on the board.
- Each learner picks three habits they regard as difficult to adopt. They write their reasons and read them out in groups. The other group members suggest what the reader could do to overcome their inner resistance, e.g. *I find it easy to get into a flow when I play tennis, but not at school. – That's because you love tennis. Try pretending you love school – for just a month*, etc. Help them if needed.
- Hand out the slips of paper in Appendix 3 to seven learners. Ask them to form a small group around them. They read out what's on their slip and the group decides which habit it refers to, and discusses any ideas it gives them.

Bathla, S. (2019) *Build A Happier Brain: The Neuroscience and Psychology of Happiness.* Kindle Edition.

Appendices

Appendix 1: Jonnie Peacock

When he was five, he was like most small boys from his home town of Cambridge – he loved to play sports. Then suddenly his life changed when he became very sick with meningitis. Jonnie's parents took him to hospital and he nearly died. The doctors saved his life, but they couldn't save his right leg. He couldn't run around with the other children any more – and he couldn't play football, his favourite sport. In fact, he couldn't do any sports at all.

But the doctors gave him a new, artificial leg. He could walk again, but he wanted to do more than that, so he started dancing and doing other sports. His doctors, his friends and his parents were all surprised that he could do so much. Only 10 months after he lost his leg, he could run, swim and play football again, but running was his best sport.

In 2010, Jonnie started to practise a lot. He wanted to go to the London 2012 Paralympics, the Olympic Games for disabled athletes. Some of the athletes in the Paralympics can't walk, some can't see at all or can't see very well. But in their sports, they can do things that most people can't.

Jonnie Peacock won gold at the London 2012 Paralympic Games when he was only 19 years old. He ran the 100 metres in a time of 10.90 seconds!

Appendix 2: Poem

What's purple?

My sister's eyeshade.

My father's car.

The cover of my diary.

My new jeans.

And the dye

I'm not allowed to use

On my hair.

Appendix 3: Habits that help create happiness

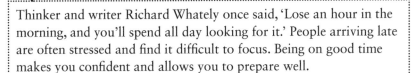

Thinker and writer Richard Whately once said, 'Lose an hour in the morning, and you'll spend all day looking for it.' People arriving late are often stressed and find it difficult to focus. Being on good time makes you confident and allows you to prepare well.

Research shows that the way a conversation starts has a big influence on the way it develops. So, make it a point to begin one by smiling, paying a compliment, finding something to comment positively on. Your partner(s) will feel good, relaxed and creative, and enjoy being with you.

You're totally involved in an activity. Time flies. You're focused on reaching your goal. You know you're making progress. Everything's easy, and you do not allow yourself to be diverted by any distractions. The more you practise this, the easier it becomes, and the more success you have.

Studies show that it's not stress itself that defeats people; it's the fact that they do not take the time needed to recover from stressful phases. Family and friends are important, play sports, have a hobby, sleep enough. And do not constantly think of what you have to do. Relax!

When someone criticises you, don't become defensive. Maybe they want you to improve? Take their feedback seriously. But learn to filter out the feedback that comes from people who want to demoralise you: avoid spending more than the minimum necessary time with them.

One person alone is limited in what they can do. So spend time socialising with people. Join clubs (or form your own), go to student meetings, support campaigns that you think have a good cause etc. This will help you make new friends and meet interesting people who'll support you when you need them.

Do good for others. When you help someone or volunteer for a job, don't expect to get something for it in return. When you do something good for someone, you will make them happy, and that in turn will make you happy, and ... remember that, and be grateful for all the good things in your life!

Index